What others are saying about "When God's Woman Wants to Give Up!"

So often I have felt alone in my trials and tribulations. Ashamed to confess the frustrations, fears & anger, wanting to quit! In this book Diane brings to us the reality through the word of God that we are not alone in the "Journey of LIFE" that God is there for us. His love is "BIGGER" than we could ever grasp. We have a purpose and that purpose is to have abundant life. — Carol Parga, Pastor's Wife, Marshall, Texas.

This book has caused me to really know that God is my Father and He loves me as an individual.

After a time when I have been angry and distant with God this book has pushed me and forced me to deal with my anger and to get into the Word of God to seek guidance and instruction. It has kept me in the word. I needed that.

The women in the Bible study felt as if they could relate to the author. The style of writing made it possible for us to relate to the her and to understand that we were not alone in our feelings of wanting to "give up." The author became a real person to us not someone in a tower that we could not relate to.

When God's Woman Wants to Give Up

Diane Nix

iUniverse, Inc.
New York   Bloomington

When God's Woman Wants to Give Up

iUniverse books may be ordered through booksellers or by contacting:

iUniverse
1663 Liberty Drive
Bloomington, IN 47403
www.iuniverse.com
1-800-Authors (1-800-288-4677)

Because of the dynamic nature of the Internet, any Web addresses or links contained in this book may have changed since publication and may no longer be valid. The views expressed in this work are solely those of the author and do not necessarily reflect the views of the publisher, and the publisher hereby disclaims any responsibility for them.

ISBN: 978-0-595-48074-6 (pbk)
ISBN: 978-0-595-51677-3 (cloth)
ISBN: 978-0-595-60173-8 (ebk)

Printed in the United States of America

iUniverse rev. date: 3/18/2009

Unless otherwise noted, all Scripture quotations are taken from the New American Standard Bible, copyright © 1960, 1962, 1963, 1968, 1971, 1972, 1973, 1975, 1977, and 1995 by The Lockman Foundation. Used by permission.

Other Bibles quoted are marked NLT, Holy bible, New Living Translation copyright © 1996, 2004 by Tyndale Charitable Trust, used by permission of Tyndale House Publishers, The Message, copyright © 1993, 1994, 1995, 1996, 2000, 2001, 2002. Used by permission of NavPress Publishing Group; NIV, New International Version, copyright © 1973, 1978, 1984 by International Bible Society; NKJV, New King James Version, copyright © 1982 by Thomas Nelson, Inc. Used by permission.

To my family.

Preston, you saw in me what I didn't see in myself. *Thank you for your daily prayers. From the first day that I met you, you challenged me in my Christian walk. I fell deeply in love with you as I watched you live your life for our Lord. Thank you for your unconditional love and your belief in me. I am honored and blessed that you are my husband.*
I love you more today than ever before!

Rebekah, you are my first child to bring home, *the fulfillment of a promise, my blessed gift.*
Rachel, you completed the promise, you make my heart glad *and cause me to smile from the inside out.*
I cannot wait to see what God is going to do in His kingdom through the two of you! I am so proud of you. I am so blessed to be your mom.

Contents

Foreword ix

Acknowledgments. .xi

Introduction xv

1-When It Feels Like All Hell has Come Against You 1

2-When Life Seems Unfair 15

3-With Friends Like These Who Needs Enemies 23

4-The BFF Factor 35

5-Who's Your Daddy? 47

6-Why Do I Need to Know My Daddy?. 63

7-Deal With It or It Will Deal With You!. 69

8-Fill Up the Empty Places 93

9-Don't Move 103

10-The Reminder 111

When We Surrender 114

Living in Balance 115

Historical Background on the Book of Job 117

Works Consulted and Sited 121

Scriptures and Notes by Chapter 123

Foreword

It is possible that you picked this book up, because you have been experiencing just what the title expresses. Are you in the midst of a frenzied, "I'm at my wit's end" kind of day? Are you facing a debilitating illness, the loss of your marriage, a rebellious child?

Life in a fallen world is not all that our hearts tell us it should be. We know that there must be an answer to our dilemma; we're just not sure where to look. Well, allow me to introduce you to the author of this book.

Diane Nix is highly qualified to write this book. Why do I say that? She has personally walked through many trials and has come out with a deeper understanding of Job's wife and why a woman who trusts God might come to the end of her rope.

Diane is a woman, just like you and me. She is a wife and mother. I have known Diane for over twenty years. She and I met when our husbands were in their seminary Ph.D. program. It was one of those "instant" connections – a kindred spirit.

I have personally walked with Diane through the loss of a child, a very difficult and painful church experience, the death of her father, helping to care for her aging mother and then losing almost all of their physical possessions three weeks after moving to New Orleans.

As if that were not enough, she then suffered a close brush with death and has come out shining like gold!

She understands that life at best is unpredictable and can be downright brutal. Instead of running from the pain, she has embraced the lessons and pushed in to touch and trust her Abba, Father.

This book, if applied to your life will help strengthen you inwardly, so that when the trials or storms of life buffet you, you will not be easily shaken. All because, the foundation of your life, is the Rock of Jesus Christ and His Word.

It is through God's Word that we are enabled to set our minds on things above and as Diane says, "we can keep seeking the things that are above when the things below are a mess and out of our control." It is here that we find our refuge and hope is renewed.

Read this book – you will be encouraged to keep on keeping on. God, the Father is calling your name. Won't you answer by delving into this book and the truths it contains from His Book. Then, may you be able to say as Job did, "I had heard about you before, but now I have seen you with my own eyes." Job 42:5

In Christ,
Donna Gaines
Author, Speaker, Bible Teacher, and
Pastor's wife of Dr. Steve Gaines,
Pastor of Bellevue Baptist Church,
Memphis, Tennessee.

Acknowledgements

Words cannot express the gratitude that I have for the people who have helped me to complete this project. When I first felt the urging to write, it was many years ago. I never dreamed that when God put the vision of this book into my heart He would have me live it out before I could put it on paper. This book is in part the journey of my life. God has placed people to intersect me on this journey and to use them in the midst of the greatest and most trying moments of my life. I have not always done well in these moments but I am grateful to our God that His mercies are new every morning. I am blessed beyond measure to have a Savior that will allow new beginnings more than once. I am eternally indebted to a heavenly Daddy who can see past panoramic vision for my life. Thank you God for saving me. Thank you for taking me just as I am and changing me and molding me into who you have had planned from the beginning of time. I know you are not finished with me but I look forward to the next days on this journey.

I could never complete this huge task without my family. Thank you, Preston, for daily praying for me. Your encouragement and continual belief in me have spurred me on to be more of what God wants me to be. Rebekah and Rachel, I stand in amazement that God has given me the two of you. Both of you are so far down the road in your walk with Christ. I stand awe at your spiritual insight and desire to walk with our Lord. I am overwhelmed with excitement to see what our Lord will do in and through you as you continue to know Him more and more.

Donna, years ago when we met you have no idea the impact that you made on my life spiritually. You continue to be the friend that drives me to the throne room of our Savior and our Abba Father. Thank you for your prayers and for your unconditional love. Thank you for your friendship. I love you. You have said that I have sharpened you. I would say that you my friend are the one that has sharpened me.

Carol, where would I be if it were not for you're your faithfulness to listen to our Heavenly Abba Daddy. Thank you for calling on heaven continuously on my behalf. Thank you for believing for me, God's best. Thank you for hounding heaven on my behalf. You encourage me and challenge me with your great faith. I love you. You have taught me how to pray with great belief.

To the first group of women at First Baptist Covington that I taught this book to, thank you for your patience, insight, and gentle critique of the work. To the women's Bible study group of First Baptist of Sapulpa, Oklahoma thank you for your words of encouragement. Northlake Christian School Elementary teachers, it was my honor to be able to speak to you about what God was doing in the midst of this writing. Thank you for letting me share part of this journey with you. Finally, to the New Orleans Seminary Brown Bag Lunch group, you were very patient with me as we continued the walk of this study and book. Thank you for your insights. I am grateful to all four of these groups that acted as sounding boards in the process of bringing the book to print.

To Mrs. Toni, I say thank you for the place of retreat and your giftedness of hospitality. Your friendship and home was a place of great focus and direction during the edit of this book. I am grateful to you and Bill for the investment that you have made in my family and me. God bless you and prosper you in the coming days and years.

I am eternally grateful to many that edited, corrected and challenged the wording of this work. To Joni, you are a faithful encourager with keen insight into the written word and to the Word of God. May God prosper you in your giftedness in the coming days. To Heather, who has a love for our Lord and insight into the written word, thank you for sitting with me and beating out the sentences. Thank you for your editing, correction and the sacrifice of your time. Thank you for the friendship you offer, I look forward with anticipation to the coming days of our friendship. Missie, thank you for your words of encouragement, editing and guidance each and every time I ask you to read a section. You are truly a "soul" sister. Finally, to Beth, you are an incredible woman of God. Never forget this. Thank you for editing this work with an eye of an editor and English expert. I am extremely grateful for the sacrifice of your time.

Finally, to my Bible Study Fellowship class and to all of the friends, new and old, those who have encouraged me to keep writing and to finish what I started, you honor me with your words of encouragement. I pray that all of us will continue to grow in our love for our God each day until He takes us home. I pray that we will never give up. But when we want to give up, I pray that each of us will not let the other stop until we get to meet our Savior face to face!

Thank you all. I love you!

Introduction

Have you ever just wanted to give up? Have you ever wanted to quit....throw in the towel.... chunk it to everyone? Have you ever wanted to disappear...or if we are really honest - have someone else disappear? Do you ever just feel like doing something else, somewhere else, with someone else? This book is to let you know that you, as a woman, are not alone.

Life as we know it is hard and there are many types of demands on women. The good news is that we are not alone. There are literally thousands of women just like you and me.

So, if you are the woman who wants to pull the covers over your head and hope that if you look again that you will be someplace else with someone else, take courage, you are not alone. If you are the woman, who cannot take another day of car pool, screaming kids, negative check balances – you my dear are not alone. If you are the woman, who has remained faithful to your marriage vows ALL these years and just found out that HE isn't, hasn't and wasn't – You are not alone! Perhaps you are the woman who has received a word from the doctor of a terminal illness for yourself or a loved one. OR maybe you are the woman that is truly alone in this world. You have no one to talk to. Your "prince charming" has not ridden up and swooped you up into the "happily ever after" life and frankly you are just sick of this single life thing. You could be the woman who is at her wits-end. You are at the end of all the resources at your disposal, and there is nothing left and nowhere to turn to make this life work anymore.

I know what it feels like to want to give up. In my own life, I have experienced the death of a child and the loss of all my material possessions. I have had more than one debilitating illness that has threatened my ability to care for my family and my life. I have had some of those closest to me betray me and reject me. I have felt abandoned by my God and completely and totally alone in this world.

In my years of ministering to women, I have seen women who have chosen to give up. I have watched them as they have simply faded into the background as life passed them by in bitterness, anger, unforgiveness, and silent pain. God's Word says we were never intended to live this way. We were definitely not intended to live in obscurity for the rest of our lives. We have a purpose and that purpose is to have abundant life.

A scripture from the Bible comes to my mind; "There is nothing truly new under the sun." [1] There is a woman that lived 4,000 years ago. We know her as Job's wife. After the death of her children, loss of all her material possessions and the loss of her reputation she chose to give up and cried out, "…. Curse God and die!" In the following pages you and I will discover that we can make a better choice.

Chapter 1

When it feels like all Hell has come against you!

What is it today that brings a woman to a place of giving up? This is the question that I have asked countless women over the last two years. Recently, I was on a plane and happened to be sitting next to a doctor who has been practicing gynecological medicine for several years. I asked her, "What brings a woman of today to the place that she wants to give up?" She did not hesitate when she answered, "Choosing the wrong man." She went on to explain that women of today look to men for the answers to their problems.

Another time, on another plane I was seated next to a registered nurse who was an officer in the United States Air Force. She was returning from a first ever conference that was held for women of the Air Force to recognize their contributions over the years. I asked her opinion on what brought a woman to want to give up. I received a very different answer. She believes that women want to give up when they lose their confidence. She went on to say that when a woman doesn't believe in herself she could come to a place of "throwing in the towel". For her the answer was to have enough self-confidence!

I interviewed several other women and their responses varied and swung like a pendulum. In fact, the answers for bringing women to a breaking point vary as much as the many various trials that we encounter along this journey we call life!

Some women today look to men to give them their identity. They have equated sex for love and that in turn has left them empty, used, misunderstood and spent. Women who look to a man for their identity are put in a spot of vulnerability that many times leaves them raising the kids, paying the bills, taking care of all of the household duties alone and with no support - financial or emotional.

The woman who believes that having enough confidence leaves herself in a place of vulnerability as well. There are times that this life will deal us such a crushing blow that no amount of our own self-will and confidence can pick us up and keep us going. She can stand on top of the mountain of her confidence and scream about her ability but if there is no one listening or no one cares; she is left with many unanswered questions.

I have lived in a time when I thought that having the man of my dreams was the answer to all of my life's problems. I have thought that if I could just keep thinking positively about my life and if I did not stop working and kept on believing in myself, it would all work out. As mentioned in the introduction Job's wife is a perfect example of living life with expectations and the confidence that what you can see and what you have gives you purpose and meaning to live life well. As we get to know her story, we will discover that life and our choices are not all about what we can see with the human eye. In reality, she was no different than you and me.

The Life of Job's Wife...

Let me tell you more about Job's wife. We find her in the book of Job that was written 4,000 years ago in a land where the women were not always honored for who they were, but because of the culture of the day were treated more as property. However, with Job's wife her life was one of great position, possession, and pride. Her husband not only loved his God but he loved her and their children. As the Bible says he was, *".... blameless, a man of complete integrity. He feared God and stayed away from evil."* These first two verses are very powerful. They set the stage for the life and story of a man, wife and his family. The next few verses reveal to us that Job has seven sons and three daughters. He owned seven thousand sheep, three thousand camels, five hundred teams of oxen, and five hundred female donkeys, and that he employed many servants. The scripture literally says, "...he was, in fact, the richest person in that entire area."[2] Let's stop right here for just a moment. What woman reading this can't understand that Job's wife had a lot to lose? She was married to the richest man in the country. She had servants, material possessions, status in the community, and great kids. She even had a good man. She was married to a man that the scriptures says, "was blameless and with complete integrity."[3] WOW! Because Job "feared God and stayed away from evil" we can know that he honored his wife and took care of his children. We know that he took care of his children because of what we are told about him in verses four and five. He had a regular practice of offering sacrifices for his children after their celebrations "for fear that they may have sinned and have cursed God in their hearts." Job was a great guy to be married to especially in the day that Job's wife lived in. Well, let's just get down with it - he would be a great guy to be married to today!

One Day...

Job's wife is married to this great guy and life is really good! It's wonderful. It's complete. Life for Job's wife would be what you and I termed a "fairy tale" existence. She was a woman in charge of a large household. She had all of her needs met. She had not a worry in the world until...

One day the angels came to present themselves before the LORD, *and Satan the Accuser came with them.* [7] *"Where have you come from?" the* LORD *asked Satan. And Satan answered the LORD; "I have been going back and forth across the earth, watching everything that's going on."* [8] *Then the* LORD *asked Satan, "Have you noticed my servant Job? He is the finest man in all the earth—a man of complete integrity. He fears God and will have nothing to do with evil."* [9] *Satan replied to the* LORD, *"Yes, Job fears God, but not without good reason!* [10] *You have always protected him and his home and his property from harm. You have made him prosperous in everything he does. Look how rich he is!* [11] *but take away everything he has, and he will surely curse you to your face!"* [12] *"All right, you may test him," the* LORD *said to Satan. "Do whatever you want with everything he possesses, but don't harm him physically." So Satan left the* Lord's *presence.*

Can you even imagine this? Job's wife is living her own life. As far as we know she is minding her own business and just living the good life when – Wham!! – Life as she has always known it changes forever because of a conversation between God and Satan. A conversation, which took place in heaven that, she and her husband knew nothing about. In one day Job's wife lost her children, all of her material possessions, her status in the community (because of the unwritten law of "hidden sin" when great calamity comes your way), and most of all her hope!

When you lose your hope, you lose your joy and when you lose your **joy, you lose your strength.** In Nehemiah 8:10 it reads, "....Do not be grieved, for the joy of the Lord is your strength.'" Can you see the progression in their lives? Can you even imagine? Some of you can. It could be that one day you are living a life that you think is going to be how you end your life and then suddenly everything changes forever. Oh, my friend, do not stop here. Please do not put down this book. Keep reading…for God has a Word for you. Job chapter one verse thirteen, "*One day when Job's sons and daughters were dining at the oldest brother's house…*Isn't that just like the life that you and I live? One day we are just going along, minding our own business, living life and suddenly everything that we have known changes forever.

I do not want you to get hung up on the fact that Satan was before the throne of God having this conversation – what I want you to focus on is that Satan, the accuser, is your enemy. Revelation chapter twelve verse ten calls Satan, "…he who accuses them before our God day and night. You need to understand that Satan hates God more than he hates you and his desire is to discredit the Creator of this universe and what better way to do it than to have one of God's own (God's highest creation) turn against Him because of a great trial. God did allow the trial of Job and wife, but evil did not come from our Holy Father. God knew Job's heart. God knows our hearts. He put restraints on the enemy and you and I can take comfort in knowing that nothing that comes our way in the form of trials and sufferings comes without restraints and a purpose.

I do know that there are times that you and I invite trials that God never intended for us, but because of our willful disobedience or because of the rebellion and disobedience of others you and I will suffer. However, in the story of Job and maybe in some of our stories – you and I could have possibly faced a trial because of a conversation in heaven.

Right now I can hear women from every corner of the globe screaming, "I do not want to be a part of any conversation between God and Satan!" I understand this, but if you are a woman of Godly character and nature similar to Job or if you are married to a man whose character is similar to Job then perhaps you too will face a Job like experience. The reality is that if you and I are very honest – most of us reading this book have all faced "Job" like experiences in our lives. It is life to have losses and failures and shame and embarrassment and deep hurt and deep grief. It is what we do with these trials that make us who God wants us to be. It is how we respond to the trials that we will be known to others as over comers or as being overcome! I want my legacy to be a Woman of God and a Woman who overcame! What about you?

So on this first, "One day" Job and his wife are stripped bare of everything that has given them meaning and purpose on this earth. In verses fourteen through nineteen we are told the details of the loss that ended with the loss of all their children. Can you even imagine? One messenger after another messenger came to deliver each message. With each message there was more intensity and with each message the gravity that their lives would never be the same. Until finally that last messenger arrives as the third one is finishing up. *"[18] While he was still speaking, another messenger arrived with this news: "Your sons and daughters were feasting in their oldest brother's home. [19] Suddenly, a powerful windswept in from the desert and hit the house on all sides. The house collapsed, and all your children are dead. I am the only one who escaped to tell you." [20] Job stood up and tore his robe in grief."* There it was - the worst possible news that a parent can receive. Nothing could have prepared Job or his wife for this news.

Maybe you have lost a child. You know the devastation of this kind of news but can you imagine losing all of your children in one day? The grief would have been unbearable. Job tore his robe, shaved his head and fell to the ground before God. He then made an amazing declaration, *"I came naked from my mother's womb, and I will be stripped of everything when I die. The LORD gave me everything I had, and the LORD has taken it away. Praise the name of the LORD!"* [22] *In all of this, Job did not sin by blaming God."*

Job understood who he was and whom he belonged to. At that moment the preceding statement of faith set the stage for the coming days of his life. He was not going to give up or quit, even though there would be times that he would cry out for mercy. There would be times of wanting to die and even days that he cursed the day that he was born. He would have no support from extended family or friends. He and his wife were beginning a journey that would change the course of their lives forever.

Another Day…

We do not know how much time passes between this "One day" and what happens next. But once again we are told in Job chapter two that God and Satan have a conversation about Job.

"Then the LORD asked Satan, "Have you noticed my servant Job? He is the finest man in all the earth—a man of complete integrity. He fears God and will have nothing to do with evil. And he has maintained his integrity, even though you persuaded me to harm him without cause." [4] *Satan replied to the LORD, "Skin for skin—he blesses you only because you bless him. A man will give up everything he has to save his life.* [5] *But take away his health, and he will surely curse you to your face!"* [6] *"All right, do with him as you please," the LORD said to Satan. "But spare his life."* [7] *So Satan left the LORD's presence, and he struck Job with a terrible case of boils from head to foot.* [8] *Then Job scraped his skin with a piece of broken pottery as he sat among the ashes."*

Can you relate to this story at all? When Job was at his lowest and it seemed that he could get no lower, he is now sitting on an ash heap scraping his boils. This ash heap was basically the dump outside of town where the town's people came and pitched all of the broken pots and trash. The ash heap is what it sounds like it is. People burned the trash and then the ashes were left. There Job sat on that ash heap scraping the boils with pieces of broken pottery and rubbing ashes in the boils to try and dry up the oozing boils.

Can you even imagine the thoughts that were running through this woman's mind? I have tried and I can tell you I would have been at my wits end. In Job chapter two verse nine Job's wife says, *"Are you still trying to maintain your integrity? Curse God and die."* She commands that Job curse God and die. She communicates this in sarcasm and utter despair. I have always envisioned her with her hands on her hips - with a really mean, fed-up, "I cannot believe what I am hearing or seeing face," saying, "Well (with a southern twang), AAR Yew still goin to trust God after all of this - well, BLEEESSSS God and die! " with a very sarcastic emphasis! (See the Historical Background on Job for information on the usage of the word bless.) I know this is not what she sounded like but there is no woman in the world like a good southern woman fed up with where she is!

Job did not condemn his wife. He challenged her. In verse ten of Job we see him reply to his distraught wife. "... *"You talk like a godless woman. Should we accept only good things from the hand of God and never anything bad?" So in all this, Job said nothing wrong."* I am convinced that this woman was not an evil woman or a faithless one – but she was a woman like you and me. She had lost everything that had given her meaning, position and status in life. And the worst possible loss, she had lost all of the children that she had birthed. As earlier discussed, if you have ever lost a child or know of someone who has – one is a devastating loss to bear at a time – she lost all of her children in the same day. She was at the very end of her emotional strength! Now she walks out to find her husband, the only thing that she has left in the world, and he is covered in boils! Those boils have worms in them, and she is overwhelmed with thoughts of despair! Can you just imagine! What would your initial reaction be? Even if you were able to get through the first test, when you walked out to see your man in the condition of Job, what would you have said about the God you had been serving along with your husband?

I know that as God gently rebuked Job's wife through her husband she sank back into the shadows. We really never hear anything else about her in scripture except for verse seventeen of chapter nineteen. *17"My breath is offensive to my wife, and I am loathsome to my own brothers."* In my opinion I believe she watched the days unfold for Job as he sat on that ash heap and dialogued with his fair weather, judgmental friends. She continued to serve him and to take care of him during his illness. He was the only thing in this world that she had left and I have an opinion that she was a Godly woman otherwise Job would not have married her. And so day and night she took care of his daily needs and she watched as the disease took its toll and heaven was silent. She watched as friends would betray him, accuse him and judge him. She watched and she probably prayed. We can conclude that she is there when God does speak with Job. She is in the shadows. I have often wondered where her heart was during this time. Was she healing? Was she bitter? Was she angry? We will never really know until heaven.

What we can know is that there is a difference between this woman and us. She did not have the revealed Word of God to lean on. She did not have a culture that valued women. She did not have a networking system to keep her in touch with Godly friends. She had no way of seeking guidance or trying to educate herself through the Internet about the disease her husband was suffering. She could not blog her emotions. She could not even use her cell phone to vent her rage. She just had her husband. She just had her God. She had a knowledge and relationship with a God in whom her trust was shaken. A God in whom she wanted turn her back on but didn't dare. A God she was going to have to reconcile with or face the consequences and I believe she understood that.

Today, right now, I want you to check your heart. Without a true personal relationship with Christ, you cannot survive these types of moments. When several years ago, after years of trying to conceive, I found out that the baby I was carrying into my sixth month of pregnancy had died and that I was going to have to deliver my baby without joy – I made a choice during that crisis to worship God and to trust Him in the moment. It was afterward, when days had gone by and people went back to their lives that I began to grieve and fight the fight of doubt and anger. God was kind and gracious during those days. My husband prayed for me and stood with me and because I had a personal, intimate, growing relationship with God – I came through.

Right now, would you ask God to search your heart? Do you have a saving knowledge of Jesus Christ? Have you come to Him, confessed your sins, and asked Him to forgive you of those sins and to come into your heart to be your Lord and Savior? If you have not – let me tell you – You will give up when times of testing come. You will have no hope. Your value for life will be completely wrapped up in those things and people around you.

Please take a moment and pray:

Dear Jesus,
Forgive me of my sins
Come into my heart and save me from myself.
Be my Lord and Savior
Thank you for saving me!
Amen!

If you know that you have an intimate personal relationship with Jesus and the Father, then pray this prayer:

Dear Jesus,
Help me to search my heart
Help me to make my value and worth not based
On the things or the people in my life, but help me to base
My life and value on who you are in my life.
Help me to place all of my hope and all of my being in you
I will trust you – no matter what
Amen!

Everything you have been reading thus far has been foundational. We needed to become a little more familiar with Job chapters one and two and you needed to ready your heart. The next step in our journey is to discover that there are lessons to learn from all our trials.

Lessons to Learn

Suffering is going to come. Now doesn't that make you happy? When we as women will embrace this fact then we will begin to not be taken so off guard by the enemy when he comes at us with yet another scheme or another temptation to just throw in the towel.

In our lives come extreme blessings and extreme trials. As maturing believers, we encounter various trials. With trials come suffering. People of all nations, but especially Americans – do not feel that we should suffer at all. It is painful and many times unfair. As American Christians many of us look at suffering as a curse word that we want to quickly and systematically explain away when it is happening to someone else. In other words, when suffering comes to a friend or a loved one we have all the answers but when the suffering comes to us – we wail as loudly or even louder as the person whom we have just given counsel. How contrary to scripture that is! In Second Timothy chapter three verse twelve the Bible says, "For those who live godly in Christ will suffer persecution." Paul, who wrote most of our New Testament, knew about suffering. In Philippians chapter three verse ten, he wrote," [10] that I may know Him and the power of His resurrection and the fellowship of His sufferings, being conformed to His death."

God does not play favorites. We will not always understand. Suffering is going to come to every person who lives on this planet. There is not anything any of us can do to change that. He knows that He is doing a work in us far beyond the actual trial and suffering. If left undone we will never reach our full potential in Christ. In the book of James we are reminded to …"Consider it all joy, my brethren, when you encounter various trials, [3] knowing that the testing of your faith produces endurance. [4] And let endurance have *its* perfect result, so that you may be perfect and complete, lacking in nothing." Suffering is not the issue – getting through it God's way is!

Life Experience cannot be our plumb line for how we will face our sufferings and trials. We have to get into the Word of God and stop using our past experiences, how we handled those situations, what talk show hosts have said, or what our best friends have said to do. We must be in prayer, seeking God with our whole heart as we pass through some of the most difficult days of our lives.

In the last twelve years, God has allowed intense purging and cleansing through fiery trials in my life. I have endured false accusations. I have been maligned, slandered, ridiculed, judged and betrayed by some closest to me. I have watched the man I am married to, the love of my life, accused falsely, belittled to the point of depression and, as he puts it, become " a gunslinger who has lost his nerve." We both have endured physical attacks upon our persons. The most recent trial of suffering for us has been the experience of Hurricane Katrina and the loss of every daily living thing. Finally, I suffered a mysterious bout of viral/bacterial meningitis that literally almost killed me.

I cannot rely on these trials and suffering to be my plumb line of whom my God is. Christ and the power of His Word must be the reason that I choose to live every day. To know my Father and to make Him known should be my goal in life. Nothing else matters. I have not always done the right thing. I have made many mistakes. I have not been still or silent. I have chosen wrongly in my attitudes and my actions and reactions. I do not know if God and Satan had a conversation about my family or me in heaven, but I do know that through some of the most difficult days God's Word has sustained me. It has been the balm of Gilead. God has been my Deliverer. God has been my Provider. He has been my Shield. He has been my Hope.

The Word of God is our manna (food). It feeds the "spirit man". You and I must feed our spirits and our souls with the "living, active, sharper than any two-edged sword," Word of God if we want to come through the other side of suffering with the Lord in grace and dignity. Second Timothy three verse sixteen says, "All Scripture is inspired by God and profitable for teaching, for reproof, for correction, for training in righteousness;" and in Hebrews four verse twelve, (NLT), we are told, " *¹² for the word of God is full of living power. It is sharper than the sharpest knife, cutting deep into our innermost thoughts and desires. It exposes us for what we really are.*" What an incredible reminder for us to feed the "spirit man." In first Thessalonians five verse twenty-three (NLT)says, "*²³ Now may the God of peace make you holy in every way, and may your whole spirit and soul and body be kept blameless until that day when our Lord Jesus Christ comes again.*"

We must attend to our spirits, our souls and then our bodies. It is the inner man, our spirit that relates to the Holy Spirit living within us. Second Corinthians chapter four verse sixteen (NLT), [16] *"That is why we never give up. Though our bodies are dying, our spirits are being renewed every day.'* We must pay attention to living our lives from the "inside out." [4]When we live life from the "inside out" we allow our spirits to come into unity with the Holy Spirit living in us. Then as we feed our spirits with the living Word of God we surrender and submit our spirits, souls and our bodies to the will of the Father.

Most Christians I know spend a lot of time feeding the body, and the soul (intellectual knowledge). The spirit may or may not get fed at all because the body and the soul take center stage in living this life. This life is called the life of the flesh. It is self motivating and self-exalting at its core. You can disguise it in religion for some time however, eventually the real true you will come forward. If we make a conscious willful decision to feed the spirit man and surrender our spirits, souls and bodies to the will of the Holy Spirit through prayer then when we begin to feed on the Word of God we can and will see victory in our lives where there has been defeat. We begin to live out a spirit-filled life that is unfortunately a commodity that is a rarity in the church today. You see, one who has a spirit filled life lives life and looks at life as Oswald Chambers expresses, "...not out for own cause at all, we are out for the cause of God..."[5]

God knows where you are and He is not going to leave you or forsake you. God sees you and knows where you are. We need to settle this in our hearts. When the trials come, if we know that our God sees where we are, it will make a huge difference in our emotional state. There is no better way to understand the truth that our God knows where we are than to read it for ourselves.

Please enjoy reading Psalm 139:1-18(NLT). *[1] For the choir director: A psalm of David. O LORD, you have examined my heart and know everything about me. [2] You know when I sit down or stand up. You know my every thought when far away. [3] You chart the path ahead of me and tell me where to stop and rest. Every moment you know where I am. [4] You know what I am going to say even before I say it, LORD. [5] You both precede and follow me. You place your hand of blessing on my head. [6] Such knowledge is too wonderful for me, too great for me to know! [7] I can never escape from your spirit! I can never get away from your presence! [8] If I go up to heaven, you are there; if I go down to the place of the dead, you are there. [9] If I ride the wings of the morning, if*

I dwell by the farthest oceans, ¹⁰ even there your hand will guide me, and your strength will support me. ¹¹ I could ask the darkness to hide me and the light around me to become night,¹² but even in darkness I cannot hide from you. To you the night shines as bright as day. Darkness and light are both alike to you. ¹³ You made all the delicate, inner parts of my body and knit me together in my mother's womb. ¹⁴ Thank you for making me so wonderfully complex! Your workmanship is marvelous—and how well I know it. ¹⁵ You watched me as I was being formed in utter seclusion, as I was woven together in the dark of the womb. ¹⁶ You saw me before I was born. Every day of my life was recorded in your book. Every moment was laid out before a single day had passed. ¹⁷ How precious are your thoughts about me, O God! They are innumerable! ¹⁸ I can't even count them; they outnumber the grains of sand! And when I wake up in the morning, you are still with me!

In verse sixteen the Psalmist states, "You saw me before I was born. Every day of my life was recorded in your book. Every moment was laid out before a single day had passed." The word picture for this verse is amazing. It is the picture of an artist taking a sketchpad and sketching out the picture that He would love to paint or draw. It is the perfect picture. When the sketch is complete he puts it on the easel and stands back to begin the painting. The Lord has a perfect picture that He desires for our lives. He knows we will make our own choices and He sees them, so the sketch is not in stone. The sketch was made to incorporate our will. And so when our sovereign, omniscient, omnipresent, omnipotent God sees that we are choosing against the initial sketch, or for that matter that someone else is altering the sketch because of their own free will, He includes that part of the sketch of our lives in the picture. Moreover, if we let Him, He will incorporate every bit of our pictures into a story to bring glory to Himself. We get to choose whether or not we will allow Him to be glorified or if we will become bitter, angry, resentful, unforgiving. We get to choose whether we are a victim all of our lives, or whether we let the God, who sees us, heal us and continue painting. God sees you and He loves you.

Finally, Suffering is not about our religion. It is all about the relationship that we have with our God and with the testimony that we are and that we will leave on those who come behind us. What will others say about how you handled your trials? That in itself really doesn't matter, but what does matter is what God says about how you handled suffering. One time a friend who had been struggling with her relationship with the Lord for some time came to me and told me that she had contracted the HIV virus from a patient that she had been taking care of in a nursing home. She was angry and she was bitter and she believed that this was all from God. As to be expected, her initial response was not one of trust but was one of complete and utter frustration with God and everyone else. As time passed this attitude prevailed, I desperately wanted her to allow God to take her to the next level in their relationship but she would not hear of it. She was adamant that if God truly loved her none of this would have happened. I remember, I had prayed and prayed and prayed for her and one day, God spoke to me and said, "Tell her that it is her choice." She has an opportunity to teach the people around her how to live with a deadly disease and how to die in victory or she has an opportunity to die alone. I told her. I don't know where she is today.

In contrast, a woman that was a mentor to me contracted a rare type of cancer. This woman loved God and loved His church. She waged war against this disease while continuing to serve in her church, lead people to the Lord, teach a science class at a Christian school, counsel, pray in small groups, journal, pray, live, love and laugh. She was a great wife, an incredible grandmother and a good mother-in-law. As her journey here on this earth, came to an end she taught me and others how to live and how to die with grace, dignity and victory! I will see her one-day.

So are you ready to complete the journey ladies? Let's go deeper into our relationship with God. I want to be a woman that will teach others how to live and then how to die

Chapter 2

When Life Seems Unfair

There are times in our lives that from a purely human perspective are just downright unfair. No matter how hard we try, we cannot wrap our minds around the events that unfold and cause such chaos and pain. There are times that we seem so unloved, rejected, betrayed and disillusioned by the God we are supposed to have an intimate relationship with that if we stay in this mindset we will never overcome. We must come to the realization and help our children come to the place of understanding that life is not fair. This life is not our home. This is not where it ends for Christians. We are just passing through on this earth. But sometimes we get stuck in our thinking that this place and this time is all there is. This is only the beginning of eternity for us. This is a blip on the screen. Yes, life is unfair. There I have said it. Let us embrace it. There will be times that it will seem so unfair and unjust that we will be tempted to throw in the towel and disappear. Or perhaps we do not want to disappear or quit, but in the midst of the unfairness others secretly pray that we would disappear or at least get some help.

There have been many times that I felt that God had not come through as I thought He would or should. There was one time in my life that I felt that God had betrayed me. I felt He was not fair in my life and I decided that I was going to let Him know this. So this particular day as I was riding my lawn mower, I began to scream my prayer to Him. I want you to get the visual. I was mowing an almost half acre of land with a two story house, a wonderful husband and a new baby. I was in a desert spiritually, but materially I had my needs met far beyond the average person. Not everyone loved me but many people did. Things were tough in our ministry and so I was throwing a "spiritually spoiled" child fit. I must have looked like an idiot riding on my lawn mower screaming at the top of my lungs at God. I was telling Him how unfair I thought He was, how my husband was a good man, and why didn't He notice that? I have often wondered what some of my neighbors thought about that day.

I am telling you this because I do not think I am the only woman in this world who has thrown a fit at God when we are at the end of our own emotional strength. Sometimes life seems so unfair that, if you allow yourself, you can sink deep into despair and depression. The pit of despair and depression is a place that no human can lift you.

When we encounter prolonged trials, our biggest problem is that we pray and ask God to fix whatever it is like we want it. Then when it takes awhile for the trial to end or things do not turn out the way we wanted, we become angry, embittered or resentful. Our focus can turn inward and downward. And if not careful, we miss what God is trying to teach us or do through us. In Colossians chapter three verses one through four it says, *"Therefore if you have been raised up with Christ, keep seeking the things above, where Christ is, seated at the right hand of God. Set your mind on the things above, not on the things that are on earth. For you have died and your life is hidden with Christ in God. When Christ, who is our life, is revealed, then you also will be revealed with Him in glory."* We get in trouble when we focus on the things below. And when we focus on the things below.... our identities become all about the events, materials and people in our lives.

It is human nature to struggle with all of the loss and trials in our lives. It is carnal nature to continue to live in this mindset. When we live in carnal nature, it is sin. Sin hinders our relationship with our heavenly Father and causes us to place our identities in something or someone else. For example, as you focus on the trial or suffering you may become so comfortable with strife, anger, bitterness, tragedy that you become more known for you trial than known for what your Heavenly Father has brought you out of. I have known a time in my life that I had been so focused on the turmoil in my life that I did not think my life was normal unless there was some drama going on. When there was no trial or suffering, I thought that there must be something wrong. My life had become clearly defined by turmoil and strife instead of the peace that my Father offers in and through the times of trials and sufferings. I did not know how to celebrate the victory of overcoming because I had not fixed my focus on the things above but continued to dwell on the trial long after it had passed.

Let us just stop and think about how unfair Job's wife might think that God had been to her. Remember she lost every earthly thing that gave her purpose, she lost her children, and she is left to watch her husband (the only thing she had left in the world) die before her very eyes. Job is sitting on top of an ash heap. I can imagine that she is standing near the ash heap. She is frustrated, angry, and for the moment without words. Job on the other hand speaks and he cursed the day of his birth. His cry of anguish and despair is great. He did not sin against God with his speech but his heart cry of both physical and mental pain was deafening to the heart of his wife. I believe she heard his heart of anguish and empathized with him. She had shared a lifetime with this man and now could do nothing to help but watch from a distance and wonder with Job why God would continue His silence. I would also wonder with Job why there was no movement to end the madness of this disease and why God just wouldn't let me die. He does not understand the unfairness of this place as he says that what he had feared has come upon him. He cannot eat, rest or sleep. He is not silent because of the turmoil in his body and soul. He cries out and I believe that his wife is watching in anguish, feeling hopeless and helpless to fix the plight that she finds herself and her husband in. It was unfair from a human perspective. This is really the core of what this book is about. - A Woman's perspective versus the perspective of the God of this universe. We must come to the place that we understand that unfairness is a part of life. It is what we do with the unfairness and how we respond to it that will cause us to prosper or to crater. Job is asking some tough questions. God can handle them. It is not the questions that get us into trouble. It is demanding the answers our way that leads us into the pit of despair.

In anguish and complete and utter despair, Job releases his torrent of words with his wife and his friends watching at a distance. All of them are totally unaware that the greatest enemy of all was watching and hoping that Job would deny his God and turn his back on the Creator of this universe.

The god of this world

We need to remember that we have an enemy. His name is Satan. We need to come to the place that we are not surprised or overtaken continually by the attacks of this enemy. He is real. He is mean. He is a liar and the Bible says in John chapter eight verse forty-four that he is the "father of lies."[4] He even lied to God about Job! It is in the book of Job that this enemy is given his name. It is Satan. The name Satan is a transliteration of the Hebrew, which means adversary or accuser.

He did accuse Job and he is accusing us today. In the book of Job his accusation occurred in the very throne room of God. The Scripture also tells us in Revelation twelve verse ten that he is accusing us day and night in the throne room. His nature has not changed from the very beginning. While we are being accused by the enemy Jesus is sitting at the right hand of the throne making intercessions for us. Get this picture. While the great accuser is accusing us we have an advocate that is interceding for us. That great Advocate is Jesus Christ our Savior.

What did Satan say he had been doing when he presented himself in front of the Creator of the universe?

Job 2:7 (NASB)[7] *The L*ORD *said to Satan, "From where do you come?" Then Satan answered the L*ORD *and said, "From roaming about on the earth and walking around on it."* First Peter 5:8-9 (NLT) is a great description to what our great enemy is doing all of the time.[8] *"Be careful! Watch out for attacks from the Devil, your great enemy. He prowls around like a roaring lion, looking for some victim to devour.* [9]

Take a firm stand against him, and be strong in your faith. Remember that your Christian brothers and sisters all over the world are going through the same kind of suffering you are."

Are you getting the picture that we have an enemy and you are not alone in your suffering? We must be aware of this. I am not advocating that you look for a demon or the devil behind every bush, but I am saying that you and I must stay aware of the world in which we are walking. We are pilgrims. This place is not our home. Our journey is hard enough just in our own every day decision-making. If we are not striving to live uprightly and to grow in our faith then we make ourselves easy targets for our enemy! So Stay Alert!

Just as our enemy is roaming and searching, the Lord is also searching and watching. Second Chronicles sixteen verse nine says,[9] "For the eyes of the LORD move to and fro throughout the earth that He may strongly support those whose heart is completely His." Remember this: the job of the enemy is always to duplicate the activity of the Father. He wants to take the place of the Creator in your heart. Be on guard! I don't know about you, but I do not want him to win in my life any longer.

Satan, the god of this world, is very active and as the time of the return of our Savior draws near, his activity intensifies. We must learn about him and be prepared for him. He is to be feared, not in the same way that we should fear and reverence our Heavenly Father, but in the same way that you fear a poisonous snake. We need to be aware of his bite and the poison he could inflict and what to do if we get bitten. If we don't learn, then we will fall as one of his victims. This is his delight. The only delight he will ever get, but a powerful victory if he can cause one of God's children to fail or give up. We will learn a prayer pattern in Chapter nine that will help us in our defense against this enemy.

Lessons Learned When all is lost

When I was a junior in high school in Missouri, an event occurred that changed our family forever. On a clear, spring day, I, along with my sisters, were in school in Summersville, Missouri. In the afternoon, I remember sitting in class and thinking about the beauty of the day. I was having a hard time concentrating on what was being taught in class that day, when suddenly, a girl appeared at the door asking for me and telling me she needed me now! I remember that she really did not even get permission from the teacher – she was looking straight at me and almost screamed the words, "Your house is on fire – I am to take you now!" I don't remember getting my younger sister. But we did and later we realized that we had forgotten our baby sister. My baby sister rode the bus home, came down the hill on that bus and got off to the burned ruins of what she used to call her home. Even today tears sting my eyes when I think of her coming home as an elementary student only to find that she had no home. I felt horrible for her.

I don't even remember the nine-mile drive to my house but I do remember coming down the hill into the valley, rounding the curve at the bottom of the hill, and seeing one wall of my bedroom standing ablaze. As we pulled up and got out of the car, the volunteer fire department, neighbors, and my mom and dad were working to keep the barn that was near the house from going up as well. Soon the final wall fell, and my baby sister got off the bus. As a family we stood in the driveway, with the clothes we had on our backs. That was it. Materially, we had lost it all. Something happened that day to my family, more than just the loss of things. We pulled a camping trailer in the driveway of our home, and that night, my mom and dad drew out on a piece of paper towel their "dream" home. We prayed together as a family that night. And in the next few months we worked together to begin to rebuild our lives. The community that we lived in was incredible to us and slowly but surely we began to accumulate the things we needed to set up housekeeping.

Recently, I have once again experience the loss of a home. My family experienced Hurricane Katrina. We lost every daily living thing due to the flooding in New Orleans. We have pulled together as a family, and the outpouring of Southern Baptists and friends and strangers has helped us to start again. I believe God has allowed both experiences in my life. I do not know as to whether they were purposeful tests as with Job but I do know that I have had many opportunities to choose, especially in the latest trial, to make the choice to not give up and to trust God for my future. Those decisions have, at times, been hard decisions, but willful decisions to let God take us to places we have never been so that He might be glorified and trusted and lifted up.

In April of 2006, after experiencing Katrina, I contracted viral/bacterial meningitis. I literally almost died. Since my recovery, I have been experiencing the after affects of this disease. I have not had worms in my boils, and I have not sat on the pile of clay pots, scraping my boils, but I have been very frustrated with the effects that a sickness can leave on your body.

As a Woman of God I have had to come to a place of making a daily choice to live in an unfair world with a heavenly perspective. I have been a miserable failure at times but victory is sweet. When I prioritize my life with God first, then my family, when I choose to encircle myself with Godly friends then I can move forward on the journey that God has for me. He wants you to do the same. Deal with the hard stuff and just realize it is not about living in a fairy tale story. It is about the testimony that you leave behind you and finishing well the race set before you.

Hebrews 12:1-2 says, (NLT)"¹ Therefore, since we are surrounded by such a huge crowd of witnesses to the life of faith, let us strip off every weight that slows us down, especially the sin that so easily hinders our progress. And let us run with endurance the race that God has set before us. ² We do this by keeping our eyes on Jesus, on whom our faith depends from start to finish. He was willing to die a shameful death on the cross because of the joy he knew would be his afterward. Now he is seated in the place of highest honor beside God's throne in heaven.

Chapter 3

With Friends Like These Who Needs Enemies

From a purely human perspective, life was completely unfair for Job and his wife. The two of them had no idea about the conversations that had transpired between our great accuser and magnificent Creator. At the close of chapter two of Job we discover that the word was spreading of the adversity of the family. Job's closest three friends meet and decide upon a time to go and see him. In verses eleven through thirteen of chapter two the scene unfolds as each one of his friends came from their own place. Eliphaz, the Temanite, Bildad the Shuhite and Zophar the Naamathite came to console and comfort their friend. They lifted up their eyes as they saw him seated upon the ash heap at a distance. The scripture says, "they saw that his pain was very great."[5] It stopped them in their tracks. They were not prepared for the sight of their wise, Godly friend. It took them so off guard that they did what good friends would do. There were no words to offer and so they raised their voices and wept. This was not a little tear shed for a hurt friend. They raised their voices and sobbed loudly. Then each of them tore their robes and they threw dust over their heads toward the sky. These actions were signs of great grief and mourning in the culture of the day. Then they sat down on the ground with him and for seven days and seven nights not one word was spoken from any of them.

As we have already stated Job opens his mouth and curses the day that he was born. His three friends listen to him speak his first words in seven days. You would have thought that after the first words of a friend in the condition that Job is in his friends would have been moved to express mercy and grace. But not Job's friends. In the next twenty-five chapters of the book of Job, his friends try and get him to understand their theological views of hidden sin and blasphemy - that God does not hurt innocent people and if Job would just confess and repent, there would be restoration and healing. Job is ridiculed for a self-righteous attitude and maligned for his motives. The three friends extol their knowledge of God and exalt their knowledge as being more than that of their friend. Based on the culture of the day I believe that Job's friends felt that he had finally been caught in his trespasses and that he no longer could continue the façade of holiness. To them, God was judging righteously Job's sin that had been hidden.

One main theme is for the three friends to get him to be quiet and listen to them. They know so much about God based on their own experience. They have watched him live his life. He can't be that good and righteous. If Job would just admit whatever it was that he had done then they could help him get right and the suffering would end. Job did what any righteous man would do. He asked questions of his God. He wrestled with the fact that he did not understand his friend's arguments against him. He pronounced his innocence not in arrogance but with a passion of a man that knew that he had done nothing in his life that deserved what was taking place at this time.

Job's friends, and I believe the friends of his wife, were like having a host of enemies at close range. I know that what I am about to share with you is graphic, but their kind of encouragement was akin to having a shotgun in your face and the trigger pulled. It kills. It does not build up. *(I Thess. 5:11)* *"Therefore encourage one another and build up one another…")*

How many times have you known a friend going through such a difficult time and because you are secretly thinking that she is getting what she deserves or because of lack of knowing what to say in words of comfort – you are just distant and silent? It happens. The friends of Job are openly judgmental and critical. His "friends" come and get up close and personal and in his business.

They watch him for seven days – I still believe his wife is on the side lines - watching – they are silent – observing thinking back on days gone by as they have watched Job sitting at the city gates ministering, offering counsel and advice, passing judgment and making decisions about other people's circumstances and sufferings.

Then they pronounce their opinions. The opinions of his friends are as narrow and sharp as a knife. They believe that their opinions are correct and there is no discussion with them. If Job will just do what they advise – this suffering will end.

Job is even farther than he was before in the pit of grief and despair and depression. He desperately desires for God to deliver him. But there is no peace in sight. If he has sinned – He wants to repent. But he cannot recall any known sins that he has committed that would cause God to punish him with such a severe judgment. He is desperate and desires for peace to come but there is none in sight and he wants to die. Job is making assumptions about what God is doing to him. He believes at this point that he is being judged harshly and falsely by His God – the same God whom he has worshipped and served in truth of heart. If this is his lot in life then Job just wants to die and he cannot understand a God who would want to let him live if life was going to be like this. He is venting and he is being truthful about where he is emotionally. I don't believe his friends can handle his honesty. They want him to give the correct religious answers. They are operating out of what they know of the day and the culture that they live in. Remember, their culture said, "If you acted according to the commands of the Lord God, He would bless you and if you sinned you were cursed and judged." There was no room for suffering apart from great consequence and judgment of sin. Job was being transparent with his friends believing that he could share his heart, his pain, and his questions. It was natural for him to assume that his friends would hear him, sympathize with him, and listen with their hearts. They did not. As women we do the same. A hard lesson for some of us is we share too freely with too many people. *Proverbs 18:24 (NASB95)*²⁴*A man of too many friends comes to ruin, But there is a friend who sticks closer than a brother.* There was a time in my life that I believed that everyone could be trusted and could be that close friend. I understand that I was naïve and even ignorant. How wrong I was. I went through a time that I was so transparent that I shared with enthusiasm and with a forthrightness that as I look back was very unwise. I put all people in my life on the same spiritual plane and place with each other. There are times that you and I have to be very careful in sharing our "HEARTS" because we do not want to cause another sister to stumble with the information that we share.

When we make a practice of venting and expressing frustration with a friend that in reality is just you sharing criticism and words of judgment – we need to understand first and foremost we are responsible before God for every word that proceeds from our mouths. *Proverbs 12:18 (NLT) 18 "Some people make cutting remarks, but the words of the wise bring healing."* The real truth here is that much of what I shared needed to be kept between God and myself. I did have a couple of earthly friends that I could have vented to but it should have stopped there. We need to establish the practice of praying more about our suffering and other's inflictions against us before we began to talk about the suffering or others involved in the suffering.

When a woman is wounded she is prone to one of two extremes. Either she is of the temperament that she vents to anyone that will listen or she retreats and pulls down the shades and fades into the background and shares with no one. Both of these women usually have a hard time being transparent with God. The woundedness and pain make it difficult to pray, as they should. When a Christian woman surrounds herself with Godly friends the friends will begin to speak the truth in love to her. They will not allow her to shrink into the shadows or continue to speak out of turn. They want her to get through her trial with victory and bring glory to her God.

They will not sit in silence and then pronounce harsh judgment with no mercy and grace like Job friends. These Godly friends will be the friends who will first and foremost pray for us and ask God to direct them in their counsel for us. I had a dear friend many years ago that prayed for me daily. It had been several years of faithful friendship when she shared with me that for many years she had prayed specifically for me in certain areas of my life. She had not spoken to anyone about these areas. I am sure that there were people who may have gone to her in frustration about some of these areas of my life. But she was silent in judgment of me. She just took them to the throne room of God and prayed for me. At the time of her sharing with me she let me know that God was working in my life and answering the prayers of my faithful, encouraging friend. I can never repay her for her prayers. I am the woman that God wants me to be in part today because of faithful, encouraging friends.

Ladies, a major insulator in our lives against giving up and fortifying our lives is to develop Godly friends. We need women friends who will sit with us silently when the pain in unbearable. We need women who will intercede for us and pray for us and not judge us critically or harshly. We need the type of friends that will speak the truth to us in love even when we don't want to hear it. Friends that will speak volumes to us by their silence. The kind of friends who will encourage us to go the distance in our journey when we want to give up. Friends that will not allow us to give up – no matter what happens. We need friends that will hold us accountable when we want to stop or to be less than what our God desires for us to be. Friends that will not have hidden agendas or their own perception of what God is doing. Friends who don't desire to control us but do desire God's best for us. Friends who will listen to the deepest darkest parts of our hearts and still see past all of that and believe the very best of what God has planned for us. Friends who bless us. We need Friends who encourage us. A woman needs friends who are faithful to the end of our days on this planet.

Proverbs 13:3 (NASB95) *3 The one who guards his mouth preserves his life; The one who opens wide his lips comes to ruin.* True friends understand that we are going to have our failures. True friends desire to encourage us when we are suffering and when we speak things we should not. A true friend knows how to bear a burden. A wise woman knows that she will have few friends in her life that she might share the deep secrets of her heart and not fear betrayal or be betrayed.

A true friend.....
GIVES ENCOURAGEMENT. *Romans 15:4-7* (NLT)
⁴ Such things were written in the Scriptures long ago to teach us. They

give us hope and encouragement as we wait patiently for God's promises.
⁵ May God, who gives this patience and encouragement, help you live in
complete harmony with each other—each with the attitude of Christ Jesus
toward the other. ⁶ Then all of you can join together with one voice, giving
praise and glory to God, the Father of our Lord Jesus Christ. ⁷ So accept
each other just as Christ has accepted you; then God will be glorified.

We need to be about the business of encouraging every woman in our life to be all that God wants her to be. Encourage your friend. Encourage the lady next to you in the line at the grocery. Encourage the woman that looks exhausted in carpool. Get your eyes up and encourage another woman to keep going. What does it mean to encourage? The Webster's Dictionary says the word encourage means to inspire with courage, spirit or hope: to spur on. How many of us need to be inspired with spirit and hope? How many women do you know need to be spurred on? [6]

Lessons Learned through a pattern of friendship

It is important to note that you and I were created for relationship. Our first and most important relationship is to be with our Creator. The next relationship is to be with other human beings. The differences between the male and female species cause relationships to be even more vital to women than to men. Friendships and Relationships matter to women.

I have the pleasure of having a young woman in my house that at the time of this writing is called a tween and very soon, too soon, will be a teen. Oh what joy, oh what a roller coaster ride we are on! The very morning of this writing on the way to school – I gave some very specific instructions to this incredible young lady. She informed me that the reason that we had a slight disagreement is that she is having a problem remembering everything I am telling her because when she gets to school she forgets! What? I very calmly (do you really believe that) explained to her that she better start remembering.

I then proceeded to seek out the reason that she does forget and as I progressed in the conversation – I saw unfold a pattern of friendship that is as old as time and very natural for a woman. You see this budding woman is very concerned with relationships. Relationships of all kinds rule her world right now. They matter immensely. They can drive her emotions to the highest points and to the lowest depths. I wonder do we really change that much as we get older. One statement keeps coming to mind –Friendships matter to women.

But don't let men fool you – relationships matter to them too. We were pre-wired differently by our "Abba" Father but we all need relationships and truly if we are going to be healthy and whole emotionally we should desire intimate relationships. I will agree that most men would be just fine if their wives were the only friend they had. In fact, the truth is some men only have their wives as their friend. We all need friends that love us unconditionally. Have you ever watched a group of grown women get together that are really close to each other and have a long history with one another? There is a lot of noise. Initially when they get together each one of them is talking at the same time. It makes me smile to think about that kind of setting. Good friends sharing their hearts, their trials, their triumphs, their joys, their hopes, their dreams, their trials, their sufferings, their answers to prayers.

Job's wife needed some faithful friends. I do not know if she had any. Maybe she did – I hope she did. As we read in scripture at the end of Job chapter one she and Job have no CHILDREN, no money, no possessions, nothing that gave her joy and happiness, no friends and no position. She is at the end of all her emotions. She could have chosen to support her husband but as we will see in the following scripture she found not only his "breathe offensive" but also I believe everything about him offensive. She was done. She might have been trying to take care of his basic needs but she was (as a friend has said to me) in a very bad place. *Job 19:13-23 (NLT)13 "My relatives stay far away, and my friends have turned against me. 14 My neighbors and my close friends are all gone. 15 The members of my household have forgotten me. The servant girls consider me a stranger. I am like a foreigner to them. 16 I call my servant, but he doesn't come; I even plead with him! 17 My breath is repulsive to my wife. I am loathsome to my own family. 18 Even young children despise me. When I stand to speak, they turn their backs on me. 19 My close friends abhor me. Those I loved have turned against me. 20 I have been reduced to skin and bones and have escaped death by the skin of my teeth. 21 "Have mercy on me, my friends, have mercy, for the hand of God has struck me. [22] Why must you persecute me as God does? Why aren't you satisfied with my anguish? [23] "Oh that my words could be written. Oh, that they could be inscribed on a monument,*

Job and his wife needed their friends to stand by them. But that didn't happen. Have you ever been in this situation? You are alone and not only that but it seems that heaven is silent too. How many of us have made it through suffering after suffering because we had friends and family praying for us and standing with us?

How women need **FAITHFUL** friends.

Forever – A forever friend is there in the good times and in the bad times – no matter how long the bad times last. There are friends that will be just for a season and we need to understand as women that not every friend we meet is going to be a forever friend. But an incredible example of a forever friend is found in First Samuel 1:3-41. The story of David and Jonathan is an example of a forever friendship. The oath that Jonathan swore to David of unending friendship that spanned the life of Jonathan and his son is an awesome example of a forever friend.

Authentic – A true Faithful friend is Authentic. She is herself. "What you see is what you get." Flattery will not be her game. She will not tell you something you want to hear just so you can be friends. She will be truthful but encouraging.[7]

A faithful friend, she is also committed to being all that God wants her to be as a woman. Not perfect – but passionate about pursuing God. She will be real with you about where she is. She will not wear a veil of deceit with you. She will not be one personality with you, another personality with another friend, yet another personality with someone else. She will not deceive you or anyone else. She will also want the truth told to her. She might not like what she hears – but she will have wisdom enough to know that if she does not hear it from a friend it might come from an enemy.[8]

Intuitive or discerning, a faithful friend is one that is aware of the events going on in her own life as well as those things going on in the lives of friends that God has placed around her. She is aware of the things in the physical realm and the spiritual realm. She might not have perfect clarity in everything but she has her spiritual ears up and she is watching and asking the Father on a regular basis to help her be aware of spiritual matters for herself, her family, and her friends. She has come to understand that the only way she can do this is by knowing and living the word of God.[9]

Trustworthy, a Faithful friend is trustworthy. She will keep your secrets and the secrets of others. She will do what she says she is going to do. You will be able to trust her with your life and the lives of your family. Today, trust is a commodity hard to come by. We need to understand that we do not need to expect that everyone has our best interest at heart. Why? Information is power.

She also is an example of putting her trust in God and not man. She challenges us to look to the Father and to let our true trust be in God – who made us and knows us. She does not lean on her own understanding

Proverbs 3:5-6 (NLT)"*Trust in the* LORD *with all your heart; do not depend on your own understanding.* [6]*Seek his will in all you do, and he will direct your paths*".

Hope, A Faithful friend is full of hope for you and for herself. She is one who has placed her hope in the Father and knows that he will never fail her or you. She has hope that God will take care of all things. Her hope is found totally in the Lord. Her hope knows that God will always answer.

Psalm 31:24 (NLT)[24] *So be strong and take courage, all you who put your hope in the* LORD*!*

Forgiven and Forgives, A Faithful friend is a forgiven friend. She is a Christian. She understands that a true friend and a friend that will stick closer than a sister is one that has been forgiven. Her primary relationship is with her God. A Faithful friend is a forgiving friend. Although we will cover forgiveness in a more in-depth manner in a coming chapter, I want you to understand that a friend that does not forgive you but keeps an account of when you failed her is not a faithful friend. She is also not right with her heavenly Father. Forgiveness is a key to true intimacy with the Father and to true friendships.

Matthew 6:14-15 (NLT)*"If you forgive those who sin against you, your heavenly Father will forgive you. ¹⁵ But if you refuse to forgive others, your Father will not forgive your sins.*

Unselfish, A faithful friendship is a friend who gives herself to others. Webster's dictionary states that the definition of selfless is: having no concern for self: unselfish. A faithful friend does not think about what she will get out of the relationship. She serves with her whole heart and expects nothing in return.

1 Corinthians 10:24 (NLT)*"Don't think only of your own good. Think of other Christians and what is best for them."*

A girlfriend that prays for you and thinks of your own good and dreams and prays for what is best for you is an incredible example of a faithful friend. A faithful friend is a friend that does what Philippians 2:3-4 (NLT) says, to do. *"Don't be selfish; don't live to make a good impression on others. Be humble, thinking of others as better than yourself. ⁴ Don't think only about your own affairs, but be interested in others, too, and what they are doing."* A faithful friend no longer lives to please herself. Instead, she lives a life marked by pleasing Christ, the one who has sacrificed all for her.

2 Corinthians 5:15 (NLT)*"He died for everyone so that those who receive his new life will no longer live to please themselves. Instead, they will live to please Christ, who died and was raised for them."*

Loving, a faithful friend loves. She is an example of Christ's love. She is a true example of what it means to have and to share the Love of Christ.

1 Corinthians 13 (NLT) *"If I could speak in any language in heaven or on earth but didn't love others, I would only be making meaningless noise like a loud gong or a clanging cymbal. ² If I had the gift of prophecy, and if I knew all the mysteries of the future and knew everything about everything, but didn't love others, what good would I be? And if I had the gift of faith so that I could speak to a mountain and make it move, without love I would be no good to anybody. ³ If I gave everything I have to the poor and even sacrificed my body, I could boast* *about it; but if I didn't love others, I would be of no value whatsoever.[4] Love is patient and kind. Love is not jealous or boastful or proud [5] or rude. Love does not demand its own way. Love is not irritable, and it keeps no record of when it has been wronged. [6] It is never glad about injustice but rejoices whenever the truth wins out. [7] Love never gives up, never loses faith, is always hopeful, and endures through every circumstance. [8] Love will last forever, but prophecy and speaking in unknown languages and special knowledge will all disappear. [9] Now we know only a little, and even the gift of prophecy reveals little! [10] But when the end comes, these special gifts will all disappear.[11] It's like this: When I was a child, I spoke and thought and reasoned as a child does. But when I grew up, I put away childish things. [12] Now we see things imperfectly as in a poor mirror, but then we will see everything with perfect clarity. All that I know now is partial and incomplete, but then I will know everything completely, just as God knows me now.[13] There are three things that will endure—faith, hope, and love—and the greatest of these is love."*

You and I are to be about encouraging and being faithful to our friends. In this life's journey it is imperative that we fortify ourselves with faithful friends. It is mandatory that you and I grow to become faithful friends. It is an unfortunate fact that many women do not know how to be a good friend. We have allowed the busyness of our lives to silence the need for faithful friends.

It is so lonely in this world without a friend to travel the journey of life. Maybe you are a woman that needs a faithful friend. Start by praying that God will send you a woman that will be as Anne Shirley of *Anne of Green Gables*, called a "kindred spirit". Ask your God to send a woman friend that will help you to grow in your relationship with Christ.

Continue to pray and believe until you know that God has sent you this friend. Be careful on this journey to seek God's direction in all your relationships. Remember, not everyone will have the same agenda and many women are unfortunately so deeply wounded that they will not always know how to have a healthy friendship. Some women will be friends like Job's friends. They will be friends as long as everything is going well and then in the most desperate of times they will turn and become judgmental, harsh and full criticism.

Remember that when the darkest of days comes to our lives it helps if we have someone with "skin on". We need a friend who will sit with us without saying a word. Women need friends who will be honest but loving. Women need friends who will commit to pray for them more than they speak to them.

Years ago I met a woman who has become that "faithful friend". When I met her, my thoughts were that I would love to be her friend. When the gift of friendship was offered, I took it. I have truly been blessed. She has challenged me in my walk with our Lord. She has spurred me on to be the Woman of God that He wants us to be. She has been that "faithful friend." She inspires me to live for God every day by the way that she lives her life. She knows my deepest secrets and yet she loves me still. I am grateful for her and I know that my successful journey through some of the worst times of my life was because she was there to listen, to cry, and most of all to pray for me. I am grateful to call her my BFF. As we grow older and the seasons of our lives change, it is interesting to see how God is choosing to use us to help impact the generations to come. She will never truly know the difference she has made in so many lives until she reaches heaven. But I am grateful that the day we met God set in both of our hearts to become friends.

We need to remember ladies, there are women coming behind us that need examples of Godly friendships. Someone with skin on that can show the way to relate to another woman as a "faithful friend" and a true, "Best Friend Forever."

Chapter 4

The BFF Factor

I was leading a weekend women's retreat in Branson, Missouri when a snowstorm blew in. I was the pastor's wife and women's ministry leader for the church. While at the retreat we had experienced a time of laughter and shopping and then a deep spiritual move of the Lord. The climax of the weekend had been a time of introspection. The challenge to us was that of looking deep into our own hearts at the places of woundedness and deep strongholds. I felt when we ended our worship time on Friday night that God was moving and that He was not finished with several lives. We were supposed to leave Saturday morning, but at breakfast the hotel manager came on the emergency intercom and informed us that the roads were almost impassable and that our journey home would be delayed another day. I saw this as God's divine intervention. There were over 300 women in this hotel and it was obvious that God wanted to do a work.

It was a great sacrifice for many women to be stranded in a hotel from their family and it was interesting to watch the dynamic change from having fun on a retreat to feeling trapped because you could not leave. God was preparing to move in this place in a way that many of the women had never experienced. It happened in many different forms. I cannot tell you all of the stories, but what I witnessed personally was awesome. I saw women restoring broken relationships and women pooling their money to pay for another

35

woman's extra night's stay. Women began to confessing their sin one to another and calling out for prayer. When I would finish praying with a group of women my cell phone would ring and another group of women would ask me to come and pray with them. God was indeed moving. He never wastes moments that seem tragic or difficult to us.

In between one of my prayer times, I received a call from a number I did not recognize. When I answered there was a familiar voice on the other end that said, "Di, this is Carol -----. Preston gave me your number. The Lord told me that I needed to pray for you this weekend." She went on to tell me how God had directed her to pray for me. It was exactly what I had been dealing with all day as I had prayed for the different groups of women. She then shared with how difficult it had been to track down our phone number, as she did not know where our family was living. What you the reader do not know is that I had not spoken with Carol in almost 13 years. We had lost contact and in the timing of the Lord He brought us back together as friends forever. The Lord did a very special thing for me that weekend. God divinely brought our friendship back together. I am so blessed to call her my friend. We have not lost contact since that time.

Women need the support of Godly Best Friends if we are going to make it through the life that God has called us to live. We need friends with "skin on" (you may need to explain this phrase) to make it through the trials, sufferings, betrayals, rejections joys, celebrations victories and just plain old life. Women of today have several obstacles to overcome in having BFF's. We live in such a fast-paced culture that there is little time for developing real BFF's much less discovering what a BFF looks like. We are programmed to believe that we need to be more than what God has intended us to be. We need to do it all and be it all. We have to keep moving and we need to be busy every minute of the day. Many women are alone with and without children and the demands on their lives to make the ends meet keep them from establishing meaningful BFF relationships. I am reminded on a regular basis of several facts about women.

1. We are BUSY – this word does not even cover what our lives are like today.
2. We are TIRED – from all of our busyness and management of our homes.
3. We are LONELY – from being busy and tired and not having the energy to develop meaningful relationships. For those of us who are married – it just takes the energy that we have left some days to focus on this relationship – who can do friends?
4. And For Some of Us – We are THROUGH trying. So we put on our happy face and we just keep going like the energizer bunny. Have you ever noticed that his expression never changes? Have you ever felt like a "Stepford Wife"?

In all honesty large populations of women live busy, tired, and lonely lives. They are ready to quit but they can't. Even in their circles of friends many women have never shared their feelings of wanting to give up. They have mastered the art of putting on a "good face" and making it all happen. But in all honesty, they are angry, frustrated, short-tempered and unfulfilled. They are quite frankly ready to explode. Most of them just need a friend that will be a BFF. But who has times for relationships!

What are we doing to ourselves? There is an old Disney cartoon where the character "Goofy" decides to go downhill skiing. There are times in my life that I can relate to him in a very big way! With no experience at all "Goofy" decides to take up the hobby of downhill skiing. He gets all the stuff that he needs to participate in the sport. Goofy attends a beginner's class – only to end up on the top of a great big peak headed downhill at record speed. Can you relate? As he skis down the mountain he gets faster and faster not only picking up speed but all different types of debris. The debris does not seem to slow him down. The look on his face is sheer terror and he keeps letting out screams that come from the very pit of his soul. Speeding down the mountain with all kinds of mishaps and rolls he narrowly escapes with his life. Has your life ever been like this or let's get real has every day ever felt this way?

The reason most women can relate to this is that we are wives or we want to be wives. We are moms, business professionals, family event coordinators, and house maintenance engineers. This means we clean the house or pay for someone to do it. We generally arrange for repair work to be done or we find a way to do it ourselves. We are washing and ironing or dry cleaner gurus (yuk!). We are the nurse (emergency first-aid giver), we are or want to be the lover of the only love of our lives, bookkeepers, lawn keepers, and landscape designers, counselor, prayer warrior, defender of the weak, and the cheerleader to the masses! Do you think that this covers our role? I am quite sure that you can add your own descriptive to the list above. The point is that the downhill race is usually out of control and would naturally cause us to shriek in sheer terror but most of us have mastered the art of making this life look normal. We know how to be overworked and overwhelmed, over everything but never letting the waking populations know about it until you "erupt."

You do know what I mean about erupting don't you? It is the steady build up of pressure from all the stuff we are doing and all the emotions that we have until, like a volcano we reach our limit and whoever is standing next to us when we blow gets not only what we have to give them right then but everything we have been holding in and holding together for the past several weeks. If we are honest we usually spew the same old stuff we have been holding onto for years. If only we would have just had a BFF to download all of our emotions. If only we could have a God centered BFF to help lighten the load and give us perspective. What a difference a friend makes!

With the role that I have just described when is there time for true meaningful friendships? We must not allow the busyness, or the hurts of hearts, or the pain of the past to keep us from reaching out for a friend that will "stick closer than a brother."[10] In other words, deal with your junk and establish some Godly BFF's. You deserve them. Relationships are part of our master design. You see our heavenly Father made us relational. We need to have BFF's.

Because of the function of our brains the Creator knew and knows that it is important for us to have a person(s) with "skin on" to share our hearts and to help us bear our burdens. When women function out of one or the other side of our brains we miss the big picture for our lives. Women have been designed to primarily function out of the right side of our brain, with feelings and emotions and creativity and friendships.

The left side of the human brain uses logic in life situations. The left side of the brain is detail oriented and ruled by the facts. This could be the reason when you try to give all of the details in a story that you might see the man in your life eyes glaze over and he checks out on you. He wants to hear just what is needed for the story to be complete and accurate. He can do without all the emotion and the extra details. Just give him the facts and he is happy. The left side of the brain is practical and safe. As has already been stated, we have been created by our Daddy God to be able to cross from the left side to the right side freely. But most of the time because of the demands on our lives women live out of the left side of our brain.

Consequently, we become agitated and irritated. In reality, if we would be free to be the women God created us to be we would use the whole person. I believe that we can conclude that part of the reason that we need friends is that they stimulate our right brain function and help us to feel whole and well.Our design by our creator is an awesome, complex, wondrous design. We live in a society that communicates to women in many different forms that we are to be like men if we are going to succeed in the world. The fruit of suppressing our need to live life from the right side of our brain leaves us without the well being of our design. When He created Eve from the rib of man, she came into being with a desire for companionship and relationships. We must get it as women – we have got to have friendships. We need the type of Christian friends that have a true relationship with our Abba Father. WE MUST have Christian friends in the day and culture that we live in. The trials and sufferings will keep coming our way. *Christian women need friends who will be honest with us and love us with a "hesed" love.*

The Word "hesed" in the Hebrew is **mercy,** an attribute of both God and good humans. Another meaning refers to the emotion aroused by contact with undeserved suffering, that is, compassion and a deeply felt love for a fellow human being. A word picture for this Hebrew word "hesed" is the picture of a loving God establishing a binding covenant or agreement between you and I. It cannot be broken. And even if He wanted to break the covenant He would not because of His nature. You can trust His Word. This is the kind of friendship that you and I need to have with other Christian women to insulate and help us to make it when the trials of life come. It is the unfailing, loving-kindness, that we all need when we are at our worst and need someone to look past the hurt, the pain, and the suffering to see who we really are and want to be. Our God does that for you and I and throughout scripture He provides examples of people living out this kind of "hesed" love.[11]

In the Bible, in the book of Ruth, we find the tale of a woman who left her country, her religion, her family, her own life and pledged to go with her mother-in-law. Her mother-in-law had lost her two sons (one of which was Ruth's husband) and her own husband in a foreign land. In the book of Ruth chapter one verses sixteen and seventeen we find an amazing statement of commitment! *"…Your people shall be my people and your God shall be my God."* Ruth left her comfort zone completely, unreservedly. What is your commitment to your friends and family? Are you a promise keeper? The statement above goes against the very nature of flesh today.

I wonder if Job's wife would have given up if she had had friends like this. What if Job's friends while sitting in silence for seven days watching him scrape his boils on the pile of pottery had begun to think not on the culture of the day, but the truth of what his life had been before this great trial. How would the story have been different if they had remained true in their covenant friendship with him instead of believing the worst when he was at his lowest? I think that it is a rare thing today to find friends like Ruth.

Mary the mother of Jesus experienced this "hesed" love from Elizabeth in a day that she should have been killed and rejected for her pregnancy. Elizabeth welcomed her into her home and provided her a refuge during the early days of Mary's pregnancy. Mary's' betrothed, Joseph, also showed her "hesed" love. Even after the angel came to him, he could have chosen, because of the law and the culture of the day, to have Mary stoned or put away. He did not. He chose to listen to the angel of the Lord and to heed what he had heard. He chose to honor his covenant binding love by taking Mary as his wife. He had no relations with her until after the birth of our Savior, Jesus Christ.

In chapter ten verse twelve of Job in the middle of his grief and anguish, Job knows that God had a covenant with him that was bound by *"hesed"* love. *"¹² You gave me life and showed me your unfailing love. My life was preserved by your care".* (NLT) Job knew that God's "hesed" love was binding and that even while sitting on the pile of ash scraping his boils he had been and still was loved with an unending, covenant binding love. He was sick almost unto death, but Job knew the heart of his God. He had spent hours worshiping him and offering sacrifices to his Creator. He didn't understand and he didn't like where he was but he knew that God loved him. That is the reason that it was so difficult to listen to his friends malign his motives and tell him who his God was. Job knew. He didn't like what he was suffering and he didn't understand, but he knew his God loved him. In the midst of great suffering Job remembered God's "hesed" love.

In order for us to understand the type of "hesed" love that Job spoke of, the reader must understand a major difference between conditional love and the "hesed" covenant binding love that never ceases and cannot be broken. Our creator instills this kind of love in the hearts of men and women. It is not contrived or worked up. It is a spiritual love that begins in our hearts the moment that we have a relationship with our Father God through Jesus Christ our Lord. This love, mentioned in the scriptural examples of Jonathan and David, Ruth and Naomi, and Mary, Elizabeth and Joseph, came into play in the hearts of people who were profoundly impacted by the love of our Daddy God.

There are many women who know nothing of this "hesed" love. These women do not have a remote understanding of this type of love. They do not have heart knowledge of the Father's love. Therefore they have their own agendas and plans for success and conditional love for their lives. Their plans may involve manipulation, control and seduction. For some of these women they are deeply wounded and have made promises and vows that they will never be hurt or wounded as they have been again.

A woman might turn her back on this "hesed" love as Naomi did with Ruth because she was so wounded from the loss of her husband and children. We ourselves can be so wounded that we become off-centered in our dealings with our friends, families and others. We might turn our backs on the "hesed" love that has never left us. It is not that this "hesed" love has left us but that we have, as with Job's wife, experienced such pain and devastation in our lives that we can lose perspective and become numb to the pain that we are suffering in trial. It is at these times we may wound others unintentionally out of the pain of our hearts. It is in these times that we feel distant from the loving-kindness of our Abba Daddy God.

In the book of Ruth as already spoken of we discovered that Ruth left her home and people and god and followed Naomi across a desert. Naomi was dejected and mournful for the loss of her husband and sons and she was in deep despair. When she entered her hometown the people cried out, "Is this Naomi?" To which she replied, "Do not call me Naomi, call me Mara (bitter) for the Lord has dealt unkindly with me. I left here with much and I have come back empty handed. I have nothing." I want you to get the picture that the young lady Ruth was with her at this point and proceeds to take care of this very ungrateful mother-in-law. She respects her and serves her because she understood that this emotional place was not who her mother-in-law was. She was in deep despair. God uses Ruth to bring her mother –in-law to a place of security. Because of this great personal sacrifice Ruth is in the genealogy of our Savior Jesus Christ.

Then in First Samuel nineteen we look at Saul, Jonathan and David. Saul was the king. After some time, God chose an unlikely young shepherd boy by the name of David to become Israel's King. Jonathan was Saul's son and by right of culture and law heir to the throne. When God chose David to be King of Israel, Jonathan recognized this, as God's sovereign will. He surrendered willingly his right to the throne to David. He pledged a covenant friendship with David and the two remained friends until his death.

Saul became extremely jealous of David. Jonathan tried desperately to help Saul come to peace with David. Saul had no understanding for the reason his son would give up the throne in lieu of David. Jonathan desired to please God more than promote himself. Saul was filled with jealously and several times when David was in his presence he would fain kindness and then throw a spear at

David barely missing him. Saul was definitely an alligator. Jealousy is very fertile soil for growing alligators. Take a look at what Proverbs 14:30 (NLT) says about jealousy. *"30 A relaxed attitude lengthens life; jealousy rots it away."*

The difference between Job, Naomi and Saul is that the first two were not involved in sin they were involved in great mourning and suffering and Saul was eaten up with jealousy. Jealousy is the green-eyed monster that can rule the hearts of men and women alike. This strong hold combined with grief, despair and great loss can cause women to turn and forget their "hesed" relationship with God. He has promised that He will love us with an everlasting love. He has promised never to forsake us or to leave us. Unfortunately today, we find many turn their backs on the God that has not left them and desires to "sustain their spirits with his loving-kindness" in the midst of some of the worst times of their lives.

Today more than ever we see jealousy center stage in many women's lives. They are jealous of what others have that they don't. They are jealous of other women's social status. They are jealous and vindictive of other's accomplishments in career, life, children, and even husbands. Jealousy can become a driving force in a woman's quest to get what she believes will satisfy her soul desires. As with Saul, some women pursue their goals with vigorous intensity and deception. This pursuit always ends in leaving her less fulfilled than before and with each failed attempt her heart hardens until she becomes used up and depleted and lonely. She will want to shift the blame for her situation on everything and everyone. Inside she rots away until nothing is left of her except a hard outer exterior and a ferocious appetite to satisfy her hunger for justification, vengeance and her own short sighted agenda. We are as Dee Brestin author of; *"The Friendships of Women"* calls an alligator or a rose.[12]

Lesson Learned about Alligators and Roses

Alligators are focused primarily on themselves and the gain that your friendship has for the course of their lives. They will do anything to fortify their mission. They will devour you and not look back in guilt at all. Take a moment and think about a real alligator. I am living in southern Louisiana right now. Alligators can be common in bodies of water in this area. It doesn't necessarily stop the locals from going swimming but just a few days ago a young man gave us a perfect example of the dangers of taking a casual swim in the bayou. Without warning, as the boy was swimming with friends a 12-foot alligator attacked and bit off this young man's arm. In a heroic fight this young man survived and remained conscious and was able to get to safety. He is now living his life without one of his arms because he got too close to where the alligators live.

It might look safe. There may seem to be no danger. But a woman whose personality is that of an alligator is unpredictable. Her motives are not pure. She is desperate to fulfill her own agenda and generally might not even be aware that she is not operating out of right motives. If you confront her she will deny it and shift the blame to you or someone else or some other circumstance. She can live in denial and deception with herself and others. She will attack when least expected and if you are not aware and careful you will not survive.

You might ask if there is hope for an alligator. The answer is a resolute YES! It will be difficult to face all of the pain and the surrounding agendas and issues that have caused her to become an alligator. She must be willing to get completely honest with God, herself, and then others. Her first step of being honest with God will be to admit to Him that she has made a mess of her life as she has tried to control it herself. She will need to seek guidance from someone who has a genuine walk with our God. The woman will need to be honest with herself. This step is difficult but crucial. It is a balancing act. The person whom she has asked to help her needs to point her to the Word of God and to the relationship that she needs to develop with her Daddy God. She must learn to see herself as her God has designed her to be without condemning herself.

God's design is one of being like a rose. As she progresses she will come to the place where she will need to begin to seek forgiveness from others that she has wounded in her life. This will also be a painful step that will need to be bathed in prayer. The timing will need to be God's perfect time. She need not rehearse the entire events but simply ask forgiveness for her wrong that she has done.

The best advice is for her to seek the guidance of her Godly friend to pray for her and to help her to know exactly what she might say. She can receive the healing of her woundedness and strongholds to become the rose that God has always intended for her to be.

A rose is living life – wanting to be right with God – but slipping up and falling at times because of the circumstances of life. She desires to be sensitive to the Lord and readily seeks forgiveness when she is shown she is wrong. She will stick you but it is not intentional. As she grows in her relationship with her God her thorns rarely harm anyone. For some of these roses, it's as if the Father removes the thorns and gives her more beauty. This kind of rose needs no protection from this natural world. Her Creator is all the protection she needs. She is therefore able to love more freely. You cannot offend her. You may hurt her but she is willing to forgive understanding that with the grace and mercy of her Father she could be where you are. She is able to give more willingly. She is truly the fragrance of Christ. She draws the deep waters out of your soul. When she leaves a room or when you are with her you know that she has something you desperately desire. The air seems lighter and brighter and you know that you have been with someone that has something special. That something special is the transforming power of the Holy Spirit living through a life that is completely surrendered to the will of her Lord. This, my friend, is a Rose.

So what kind of friend are you? Are you like Job's friends or are you like Ruth and Jonathan? Have you pledged "hesed" covenant love for your friends or do you offer conditional love for your friends. When we are faithful friends, giving encouragement and loving-kindness then we not only fortify the lives of the women that we call friends but we fortify our own lives to withstand the trials of this journey.[13] Many women cannot offer this kind of loving covenant relationship because they do not understand the Father Heart of God. They do not understand that to be loved by the Heavenly Father is to come to understand that this is all that matters.

In the next few chapters we will take a path of discovering who our God really is. I believe that part of the message of Job is and was that God is not inactive or distant from us when we are having trials and suffering of great magnitude. As we have discovered in the earlier part of this book God knew exactly who Job was. He knew him intimately. He was well acquainted with this righteous man and his worship practices. God did not allow the trial and suffering to destroy Job but to prove to the great liar the heart of this Godly man.

As a woman of God, you and I need not only to fortify our lives with Godly friends who will be faithful to us during the hardest times of our lives, but will also exhort and encourage us to deepen our relationship with our Daddy God.

Our first priority as a Christian Woman should be to mature in our relationship to Father God. Venture into the Scripture to discover all that we need to know about our Father God. He is not a distant God. He is not a silent God. He is not waiting for us to mess up so that He can judge us. He has a desire to have an intimate relationship with us. He wants us to know how to receive His love. When we receive His love, we must not only believe it (have intellectual knowledge of it) but we must, **must** embrace it into our spirits. Then as we allow the truth of whom our Daddy is we will have a healthy emotional and psychological soul and then our relationships can become healthy. As we allow the truth of whom our Daddy is we will know that when we are struggling to make it through a trial or suffering He will be faithful to us no matter what. We will know that He is aware of where we are and what we are experiencing. He loves us so much. He is first and foremost our Father...Abba... Daddy.

Psalm 12:2 (NLT) Neighbors lie to each other, speaking with
flattering lips and insincere hearts.

Romans 16:18 (NLT) Such people are not serving Christ our Lord;
they are serving their own personal interests. By smooth talk and glowing words
they deceive innocent people.

Proverbs 27:6 (NLT) Wounds from a friend are better than many kisses from an enemy.

Chapter 5

Who's Your Daddy?

Many years ago my husband and a very close friend had an opportunity to go to Israel. It was an incredible experience for both of them. Every morning before leaving for the day they would eat breakfast in the hotel. It was served buffet style. One morning as my husband had just sat down to eat his breakfast, an orthodox Jewish father and his small son walked into the room. The father was dressed in the traditional Jewish fashion. They both wore black jackets, black pants, and white shirts. The little boy was very young and the father seated him and went to the buffet to survey the breakfast and to fill their plates. Preston was seated with his back to both of them. Suddenly the little boy began to call out softly in Hebrew, "Abba.", then a little louder, "Abba!" And finally, he cried out loudly, "ABBA!" Preston at that moment heard the Holy Spirit speak to him, "This is the way that you may call to me." This is what is meant in the scripture when in Romans chapter eight verse fifteen it says, *[15] For you have not received a spirit of slavery leading to fear again, but you have received a spirit of adoption as sons by which we cry out, "Abba! Father!"* We have been adopted into the family with all of the rights of a birth child. This adoption has taken place through the sacrifice of Jesus Christ our Lord on the cross and our accepting this sacrifice as the payment for our sin, which has separated us from the Father's love. It is His plan for us to receive Jesus so that He may show Himself

47

as our true Abba, Daddy, PAPA, God! So in the next few pages I would like to introduce you to your Daddy. He is waiting for you to know Him better. He has loved you from the beginning when he "formed you in your mother's womb... and ordained your days before one of them came to be."[14]!

Sylvia Gunter the author of *Prayer Portions* says this about our ABBA, *"Our heavenly Father is always there for us. This is a reality that every person can receive supernaturally by His Spirit. Abba-Father, Papa God, is there for me when I sin...when I fall...when I fail...when I hurt...when I feel abandoned...when somebody dies...when I am uprooted and have been moved into an uncomfortable environment...when I am rejected...when I am hurting...when human love is conditional and performance-based...when life is not fair...when situations seem hopeless...when I feel dumb...when people are unfeeling and difficult ... when a friend betrays me...when the kids leave holes in my heart as they go off to college one by one...when people are too busy and insensitive... when life's demands are too overwhelming."[15]*

When Job was sitting on the ash heap scraping his boils with the pottery and defending himself against his friend's false accusation and religious platitudes he could not reconcile what was happening to him at that moment and why the God he had worshiped so devotedly was now seemingly silent. In all of his anguish however, he never sinned with his lips against his God. He asked hard questions. He wanted to die. He was angry that his friends were falsely accusing him. He made his case before the high court of heaven in his discourse with his God and before his friends. He waited for God to intervene, speak and deliver. And there is the rub my sister. We hate waiting for our God to come through for us. It is hard for us to understand if He loves us so much why He waits so long to answer our suffering or trial.

In the meantime those who are religious around us usually have the answers. We can become impatient and miss the very presence of our Father coming to us. We must spend time in our busy lives to get to know the Father's Heart for us. He is not unfeeling. He has a plan. I know that if you and I can discover His Heart for us then when the trials come as they did with Job we will wait knowing that our God is actively working on our behalf even when we cannot see it, or feel it, or touch it. We will know because we have fed our spirits with the truth that He is a good and perfect Father and nothing goes unnoticed by Him.

The Devoted Father

In the world that we live in today the word *devoted* is used very little in our vocabulary. It is an even sadder commentary that the term "*Devoted Father*" is used even less in our vocabulary when used to describe a daddy and his relationship to his children. What does it mean to be devoted? When looking in the Merriam-Webster's Collegiate Dictionary the word devoted is an adjective characterized by loyalty and devotion. When we look at the New American Standard Bible Lexicon we discover that many times the word devoted is translated, complete, safe, dedicated and peaceful. It is also translated: the mutual bond between a parent and a child.

We see an abundance of earthly fathers that are devoted to many things besides their children. I believe that it is vitally important to know and to understand that our Daddy God is devoted completely to his children. He has chosen us and is devoted to our safety, our completeness and our peacefulness. He has a bond with us through his Son Jesus Christ. He sacrificed His Son for a relationship with us and we can KNOW that His devotion will never cease no matter how many times we mess up or how many times we fail to acknowledge His devoted heart. He remains our Abba, Daddy God who loves us.

We no longer need to be enslaved to what we did not get on this planet in the way of Daddy's love from an earthly father. We can KNOW - not just intellectually - but be assured of emotionally and spiritually that our Daddy God is forever devoted to us. He has a plan for us. He knows when the trials, pains, and sufferings come that He will continue to be devoted to us even when we turn our backs on Him.

In Romans 8:15 (NASB95) we read, *15 For you have not received a spirit of slavery leading to fear again, but you have received a spirit of adoption as sons by which we cry out, "Abba! Father!"* We do not need to fear. He is with us and He hears the cries of His daughters. There may be times that it is silent but He is not inactive. He is always working on our behalf to bring us through the trial or suffering. Remember we are His highest creation. He desired to have a perfect Daughter/Daddy relationship from the beginning of time. When that did not happen because of Adam and Eve in the garden of Eden He already had the plan we find in Galatians 4:4-7 (NASB95) *"But when the fullness of the time came, God sent forth His Son, born of a woman, born under the Law, ⁵ so that He might redeem those who were under the Law, that we might receive the adoption as sons. ⁶ Because you are sons, God has sent forth the Spirit of His Son into our hearts, crying, "Abba! Father!"⁷ Therefore you are no longer a slave, but a son (daughter); and if a son, then an heir through God. Don't you see? We are heirs not slaves."*

At the beginning of this section I gave you the definition of devoted according to the dictionary. It included loyalty. Do you see in just the last few verses that we have looked at how loyal He has been to us? He has never failed us. He has made plans from the beginning to offer us an intimate relationship with Him. But as we continue to look at His heart for us I want you to understand that we have a decision to make. Will we let Him be our Daddy or just a religious icon? It's our decision. I will tell you from experience that if you serve an icon you will work yourself to death and always feel as if you have never done enough. You will also feel unfulfilled and continually needing to do more for approval. But if you begin to let Him be who He has always been then you will discover a Daddy whose devotion will never change nor ever waver.

My Defender

With Job and his wife they did not have the recorded Word as you and I do. Therefore, Job knew intimately of his God because he spent time with Him in worship and intercession for his family. His heart was right before his God and because of this Job knew that his Father God loved Him. In scripture we are told that the Lord goes before us and he fights on our behalf. Can you imagine having someone fight for you? (Deuteronomy 1:30-31) And in I Samuel 17:45-47 when David is about to fight Goliath,

David declares, "*... that the battle is the Lord's and He will give you into our hands.*" Isn't that an awesome thought! Our battles are the Lord's, if we will just let Him have everything. I know that it is difficult to let Him have control but when you and I recognize that He is fighting for us and He knows the big picture; shouldn't that release us from trying to control and manipulate our own victory? He is fighting for us and for His glory. He will defend us because He loves us. He wants the best for us and He wants victory for us. When we win – He wins. He will use the trial to purge and purify us. It will not always turn out the way that we want it. But if we get our eyes off of just what we want and desire to allow Him to defend us the victory will be better than what we could ever imagine.

Our God will fight for us. (Nehemiah 4:20) He doesn't just fight for us when we deserve it. He fights for us when we are at our worst. In the midst of the greatest battles of our lives when we are depleted and downright frustrated and not very cooperative He is fighting for us. We make it difficult for ourselves when we will not submit to the purposes of our Father. If we let Him, He will stand with us and strengthen us in the midst of the trial and suffering. He will allow us to proclaim His faithfulness and He will rescue us in his timing from the lion's mouth. He will rescue us from every evil deed and He will bring us to His heavenly kingdom. (2 Timothy 4:17-18).

Our responsibility is to surrender our own agendas and allow Him to defend us. It is a sheer act of our will as it was with Job's to lay down our own pain and suffering and our lack of understanding and let our God be our defender. Jesus was a perfect example to us. He could have put a stop to the accusations that the Pharisees laid against Him. He could have stopped the brutality of His crucifixion. He could have said to His Daddy, "I am not going to do this." But He didn't. He laid down his rights and allowed the will of God to be completed. And then when it was finished, Jesus sat down at the right hand of the heavenly Father. Jesus is still there today making intercession for us. GOD IS FOR YOU! He is not against you. HE FIGHTS FOR YOU! HE WANTS YOU TO WIN!

My Deliverer

When we are in the midst of a great trial and suffering usually our primary goal is deliverance. We just want it to be over. As Christians in this American culture we don't want to suffer long. We have bought into the lie that to be a Christian is to be blessed and without pain. The culture of Job's day was not that much different. The focus should be that no matter how long it takes, we have a deliverer. He is actively working to deliver us. We can look up where our help will come from. We need not look to the left or to the right. We can't get caught up in the logic of man or the latest religious game. Our help comes from the Lord and the Lord alone. He is the one who made the heavens and the earth. Do you want your deliverance to come from anywhere else? He never sleeps. He is your shade when it's too hot. Get in the shade girl! Praise Him for His deliverance. It is coming! He is going to guard you from rear and in the front. Acknowledge that He alone is your deliverance! (Psalm 121) In the world that we live we have been reprogrammed to fix things ourselves. But our self-help usually lands us in more dire straits. Keep your eyes fixed on the Lord. He is our deliverer.

When Jesus walked this earth He did not ask the Father to take us out of the world but to keep us from the evil one. (John 17:15) In John 16:33 Jesus told his disciples that in this world they would have trouble. Can you believe it? Why are we surprised when trials come? Jesus went on to say that we are to take courage because He had overcome the world. Do you understand if you and I will allow our deliverance to come from the hand of our Father it will be complete and perfect. It will not be unfinished or botched or contrived but perfect. You and I will be whole when the deliverance comes from our Lord. He is faithful. He will strengthen us and He will protect us from the evil one. (2 Thessalonians 3:3) When we are tempted to stray like sheep we need to return to our Shepherd and our Guardian of our souls. (1 Peter 2:25) Our Deliverer sees our troubles. He is not blind to anything that touches our lives. He has a plan. I know that sometimes it seems that life is unfair. I know that there are horrific things that have happened to you. He has grieved those things. Many of the sufferings that have occurred were not His perfect will, but in and through all of these things if we let Him He will be our deliverer and bring good out of the tragedy and pain. He will then set our feet in a large place of peace and rest. (Psalm 31:7-8)

Dependable Dad

There is almost nothing that is dependable today. Even in the best of situations people and plans fails us. But our Daddy God is as dependable as the morning sun rising. He made a covenant with us through Jesus Christ. He will never break this covenant. It is a binding agreement. (Psalm 89:3)

In a world where fear can reign on a regular basis we can take courage and act not in fear but with courage that the God who calls us his daughters will never fail us nor forsake us until our days are complete on this earth. (1 Chronicles 28:20)

We live in a world where contracts are broken every second. A man's word is not worth much. But our Daddy God is dependable and His Word is sure and true. He cannot break off His loving-kindness from us. He will not deal falsely with us. He is the truth. He is not a liar; therefore He will never alter the truth of His lips. (Psalm 89:33-34). Our Daddy God is a compassionate God. He is not going to fail you or destroy you no matter how it might feel at the moment. (Deuteronomy 4:31)

Our Daddy God's Son Jesus will never separate His love from us. Not tribulation, or distress or persecution, or famine or nakedness, or peril, or sword. He promises that though we are being put to death all day we will overwhelmingly conquer through Him who loves us. I know that some of you want to die. I know that it feels as if you are dying. And for some of you - you are dying, but God is at work! Nothing will separate you from the Love of God, which is in Christ Jesus our Lord. Death will not separate you. Angels will not separate you. Demons will not separate you. Not the trial or situation at the moment or the future will separate you. Not any power or created thing will separate us from the love of our dependable Daddy! (Romans 8:35-39)

He is our great shepherd and we are His sheep and our dependable daddy will not allow us to want. When life is good and we are walking in green pastures and He is leading us by the still waters. He is restoring us. He will lead us and teach us during this time of peace in the area of righteousness for His sake. And when the trial and suffering comes and the shadow of death is around us we will not fear for we will know that He is with us. He is delivering. He will be with us during times that we must face our enemies. No matter how dark they are. No matter the pain. He is there; delivering us. We do not have to fear for He is with us. (Psalm 23) My Daddy is dependable in the area of all my needs. He will make sure that I have everything I need according to the riches of His Son Jesus. (Philippians 4:19). My job is to honor Him with everything that He gives me. He is to get the first of all that He gives me and I must acknowledge that He is my supplier. (Proverbs 3:9)

Doting Daddy

When you think of a "Doting Daddy" are you like me? I think of a daddy who pays close attention to me. He is someone who doesn't let a detail pass by His children. He is concerned with everything in our lives. He is with us in the quiet moments and in the turbulent moments. Our Doting Daddy is with us to make sure that we have plenty. (Psalm 23:1-2) He will carry us when we need carrying. (Isaiah 40:11) He knows when we can't take another step and if we will throw ourselves onto HIM, He will carry us. It is an act of our will to let Him pick us up and carry us. Lift your arms up and He will carry you.

We are redeemed through His Son. He held nothing back. He lavished His grace upon us through the shedding of His Son's blood. He has forgiven everything we have done and everything we will do. (Ephesians 1:7-8)

This Daddy never changes and so you and I are safe and secure. (Malachi 3:6) Every good thing that is given to us and every perfect gift is from the hand of our Doting Daddy in whom there is no variation or shifting shadow. (James 1:17) Because our Daddy never changes His Son never changes either and this gives us security in our relationship with a good and perfect Doting Daddy. (Hebrews 13:8) He set His affection on us and loved us and chose our children and us. He loves US and that will never change. (Deuteronomy 10:15)

Daddy's Love

Do you know anyone who doesn't want to be loved with a love so intense that no matter what they do or don't do - the love is constant, never ending, desiring the best, deep, abiding, never ending, faithful, kind, never ending, hopeful, tender, never ending, full of mercy, grace, never ending – this love never fails?

He has so loved the world that from the beginning He had a plan to provide for intimate relationship with His Highest creation. He provided the greatest sacrifice through His own Son Jesus Christ. Jesus died for us willingly so that we might know the Daddy's' perfect love for us intimately eternally. (John 3:16) When we choose to allow the trials and sufferings of our lives to cause us to hate and to stop loving then we will not know God. For God is love. He is the essence of love. He is the definition of love. Love is not just an emotion but mainly an act of our will. When we love as God loved us and sent His Son then we understand love. He loved us so much that He provided a way of forgiveness for our sins through His Son Jesus Christ. (1 John 4:8-10) When fear rules our lives we do not know the Father's love for His perfect love casts out fear. He knows that we suffer punishment with fear and when we are fearful of punishment we cannot know His perfect love. (1 John 4:18) His love is perfect and we can know that when we are being disciplined by this perfect love that we do not need to fear for He will bring us forth in His glory.

A Daddy who stays

Today people who make commitments of fidelity and trust are hard to find. When most people stand before God and a host of friends and pledge their love to another to stay and love and never leave there are conditions to this commitment. Children have been greatly affected by the absent Father. The absent Father has come in many forms. The physically absent father is one form. The abusive father is another form. But I believe that the most damaging of all is the father who stays in the home but checks out emotionally and never blesses his wife or his children with the role of his headship and his rightful spiritual duty of blessing and leading his family in the ways of the Lord. Therefore he, his wife and his children do not understand the Daddy's commitment of faithful love. We will look further at this subject in our next chapter.

I believe that knowing and understanding that there is a Daddy that will never leave will help us as we walk in a life full of trials and suffering. He will not leave us no matter how difficult we become. He might be silent. But the moment that we confess our sins He will remove our sins and remember them no more. He never deals with us according to our sins but will remove our sins from as far as the east is from the west. He will never desert us nor will He ever forsake us. He is compassionate to us and He will never fail us or destroy us, nor will He ever forget us. (Hebrews 8:12) So far has He removed our transgressions from us. (Hebrews 13:5)(Deuteronomy 4:31) Our Daddy who stays with us goes with us wherever we go. We can be strong and courageous because the Creator of the universe by His Spirit is with us in the details and sufferings, trials, victories and happy times in our lives. (Deuteronomy 31:6) It pleases Him to stay with us. He will never, never abandon us because of his great name. (1 Samuel 12:22) Our Daddy cannot lie. This means that if He says that He is with you, He is. He will not break His covenant with you because lying is not a part of His nature or character. He is going to always be with you through everything you go through in life. (Psalm 89:33-34). This Daddy who stays is not like an earthly father nor is He a son of man that He should have to repent. He is perfect and we can take Him at His word. He will not lie to us. He says by His spoken Word that He will never leave us or destroy us and we can take refuge in Him. He will never change His mind about us. We are precious to Him. He is a perfect Daddy. (Deuteronomy 4:31; Hebrews 6:18; Numbers 23:19; 1 Samuel 15:29; Titus 1:2)

Daddy's Discipline

Have you ever had a spanking from God? None of us liked to receive discipline when we were growing up. For some of us that discipline was not done in love nor was it fair or just. Women across the world have received discipline at the hand of a father who was harsh and unloving in discipline. Many times this discipline was filled with rage. I want you to see how a good Daddy disciplines us.

When a good Daddy disciplines us it is for our good and so that we truly know that He loves us. If He left us to our own way and ourselves it would not be real love. Who wants to be around a "spiritually spoiled" child? (Proverbs 3:11-12) If we are not disciplined then we will not be able to say that we are truly the Lord's children. He disciplines us for our good, so that we can share in His holiness. Discipline is never fun and sometimes it is very sorrowful but if we let it have its way it will produce a great harvest of peaceful righteousness. (Hebrews 12:6-11) He is perfect and He knows what we need in the way of discipline better than anyone on this planet. He is just, righteous and faithful. He is the Rock. He is the only one that truly knows our hearts and we can absolutely trust Him. (Deuteronomy 32:4)

A Daddy I Can Trust

How many times have you had trust broken? If you are like most of us we can't count the times on one hand. When your earthly father - who you can physically see, breaks your trust - it will make it harder to trust the heart of a heavenly Father – who you can't see. Today more than any other day – trust is a very rare commodity. But what I want you to see is that your heavenly Father is a Daddy that is trustworthy. He will never break the trust that you have in Him.

We no longer need to live in fear. We can put our trust in him and never fear again. What can men do to us when our God is for us? (Psalm 56:3-4; Psalm 56:11) Because Jesus, our Daddy's Son, loved us as much as His Father loved us He died for us and He rendered powerless the evil that had power over us in death. We no longer have to fear death because our Daddy took care of it. We can know that we will never die a spiritual death because of what our Daddy's Son did for us (Hebrews 2:14-15; John 11:25-26)

If we seek Him we can know that we can put our trust Him and that He rewards those who seek Him. Once again, our Daddy lets us make a choice. We can stir up strife during our suffering and be prideful and arrogant or we can prosper, as we trust our Lord. We can put our trust in man and be cursed and we can make flesh our strength, or the Lord can bless us. We can be like a tree planted by the water's edge as we stretch out our roots when the heat comes and we will know that He can be trusted to nourish us in the driest of times. As we trust our Daddy wewill produce fruit in the driest of times of our lives. (Psalm 9:10; Proverbs 28:25; Isaiah 12:2; Jeremiah 17:5-8)

My Daddy full of Grace

At the time of this writing we had a new puppy in our house. She is a Pomeranian and Boston terrier mix. She is very cute but also very active and pretty destructive many ways. Well, she decided that she was going to hide from me. She is still small enough to squeeze herself underneath the china cabinet in my dining room. It is dark, cramped and small under there. She wouldn't come out. She knew she would be in trouble and she decided she would just stay where she was. I was sitting at the end of the dining room table typing this lesson and realized that her actions are much like ours. We have a Daddy who is willing to offer us grace and unconditional covenant binding love and we for our own reasoning would rather limit ourselves to a dark, cramped, small place because we think it is safer just to stay there instead of coming out into the light of our Daddy's true love and grace. We would rather live in limited freedom and much pain than go ahead and come out into the light of our Father's love. As you have been reading and discovering, pain and trials are a part of life and yet many times we would rather live in the darkness of the pain or the trial or sin than to allow our Daddy to discipline us if necessary and then to love us extravagantly. It is a lot brighter and bigger and freer to be in the presence of a Gracious and loving Daddy!

What is grace you might ask? It is undeserved favor and mercy. I heard a definition a while back. Grace is God giving us what we don't deserve. Mercy is God not giving us what we do deserve. Our Daddy God full of grace and mercy gave us His Son for the payment of our sin. We have a relationship with Him because of His grace. We can trust Him and know that His grace and compassions are new every morning. Great is His faithfulness. He is a gracious, Holy Daddy God. (Psalm 11:4; Lamentations 3:22) We are no longer under the Law but under grace. In other words we do not have to perform to have our Daddy's grace. It is by grace that He has redeemed us. We do not have to do one more thing to get redemption. His grace is enough for us. It is complete. (Romans 6:14; Ephesians 2:8; 2 Corinthians 12:9)

In this Chapter I have attempted to introduce you to a few of the endless character traits of our Daddy. I have purposefully filled the pages of this chapter with many scriptures. You and I need to know that our relationship with our Daddy is not just based on how we feel at the moment, but it is based on the Word of God that will never change. Our emotions may change by the second. Therefore as we feed our spirits, souls and minds with the truth of the Word of God it becomes not about how we feel but about what we **know** of our Abba, Daddy God. The Word of God is inexhaustible in telling how our Father desires to relate to us. He is the answer for every need we have. He has every character trait of the perfect Daddy. He desires for us to know Him more and more until our journey this side of heaven is complete. *"Now may the God of peace Himself sanctify you entirely; and your spirit and soul and body be preserved complete, without blame at the coming of our Lord Jesus Christ."* I Thessalonians 5:23.

You see we have no excuse in not getting to know this Daddy except for our own willful stubbornness. Job's wife did not have this revealed Word. You and I do. Get to know your Daddy ladies. You will not be disappointed. It will take some work but it will be worth every moment and every sacrifice. And when we are faced with the trials of this life, don't you think you will fare better if you know that you have a heavenly Abba, Daddy who is for you? Remember, He Loves YOU!

Lesson Learned about my Daddy's Love

We had just had a big day at the beach. We had come in and showered and eaten dinner and then it was out the door for the night adventure. With nets, buckets and flashlights in hand our family went out of the door for the very first time of night crabbing.

My youngest daughter was four years old and she had been playing all day at the water's edge. Rachel was chasing the waves, looking for seashells, making sand castles. She loved coming to the water's edge and letting the waves come crashing in. She would run backwards to keep them from getting her and then sometimes she let them catch her on purpose. She was fascinated with the continuous movement of the water.

This night as we marched across the wooden deck that crossed the dunes to the beach she was holding her daddy's hand. My oldest daughter age six at the time was running a few steps in front of them and I was bringing up the rear. There was an air of excitement. We were charting new territory. The beach was pitch black except for an occasional flashlight focused on the sand tracing the steps of an escaping ghost crab. The sky was lit with twinkling stars and all that could be heard were voices of children and parents already experiencing the night on the beach and the continuous sound of crashing waves hitting the shore. Rachel, in awe of all that her senses were saying to her asked, "Daddy, When does He turn it off?" Her Daddy answered, "Who turn what off Rach?" In her biggest four year old voice, "God, When does He turn the waves off?" I held my breath, held in a chuckle and Preston answered, "Baby, God doesn't turn the waves off. They never stop. They keep coming the same way at night as they do in the day." He went on to explain to her as best that he could in four-year-old language that the waves were necessary for the earth to be healthy. That God, our Father Creator, had made it so and so it was. She was satisfied. She was quiet and I knew that in her mind she was processing the fact that there wasn't a switch to turn the waves off. In her child's mind she really didn't need any other explanation other than her daddy told her that God didn't turn it off and that He made it that way.

Ladies, our Daddy says He loves us and no matter what - we cannot turn that off. God does not have a switch to turn off His love for us. His love keeps coming the same way in the day and in the night. It is constant. It is forever. It is awesome. Sometimes it's fierce and intense. Sometimes it is gentle and ebbing. Sometimes He lavishes it on us wanting us to receive it and to know His Heart for us. When we will just accept the fact that He loves us, life and trials take on a whole different perspective. We can know that nothing will touch us that the constant love of our Father is not aware of. We can take refuge in plunging into the middle of His love and letting it draw us deeper by knowing Him more. Let the wave of His love wash over you.

Chapter 6

Why Do I Need to Know My Daddy?

In the world that we live in today, the importance of intimately knowing your heavenly Father is, in my estimation, vital to a Christian. I believe how we view our heavenly Father directly impacts how we deal with every area of our lives especially the area of suffering and trials. If you and I believe that we have a heavenly Father that is silent, distant and uninvolved in the trials and sufferings, or for that matter, the very daily routine of our lives, then we will be more likely when the fire is hot and the suffering is intense to want to give up. The worst response, and typical of a woman, is to take over and fix it ourselves!

If you have had an experience with an earthly father that was negative or abusive in any form, would you be likely to trust a heavenly Father who you can't see? It is a proven fact that young children form opinions of their heavenly Father at least in part by the way their earthly father relates to them. So it stands to reason that the impact on our nation in the area of divorce has caused the absence of a father or father figure in the lives of many. I believe that this is an indication as to the reason that we struggle with our view of our heavenly Father. In a survey that Barna research conducted by phone in 2001 it was discovered that marriage is not as stable a relationship as it once was. Among the seventy-five percent of the people interviewed that had at one time in their lives been married, one-third had experienced at least one divorce. It seems clear that young adults are rewriting the rules concerning relationships and marriage. A majority of married Busters (a person between the ages of 27-41) lived together prior to their marriage. If the existing scenarios between living together and higher rates of divorce persists, we can expect to see a continued deluge of divorces in coming years, in spite of the fact that teenagers and college students have listed the desire to get married and stay wed to their spouse for the duration of their life as one of their top goals in life.[16]

It stands to reason with the given stats above that most adults or even their children would not have a healthy view of what an earthly Father is supposed to look like. If the holy institution of marriage isn't making it in the Christian or the non-Christian world then it is going to be difficult for children to have a healthy view of a heavenly Father. And if they do not know what an earthly Father (whom they can see) is to look like, then how much more difficult would it be to understand and to accept a heavenly Father and His plan and His sometimes hard to understand ways of dealing with our lives?

Trust of the heavenly Father is difficult even when you believe He will take care of you as seen with Job. What if you have never known a Father's unconditional love? What if your Father was absent? Sylvia Gunter, founder of *The Father's Business* and the author of *Prayer Portions*, shared with me several years ago that she believes there are three types of damaging or hurtful Daddies. These earthly daddies directly impact and affect how children of these homes believe the heavenly Father views and accepts them.

The first father Sylvia describes is simply the absent father. He is not physically present for the child. He leaves, abandoning the family and never looks back. He never or rarely takes an active role. Responsibility for the raising of the children is left mainly to the mom or someone else.

Secondly, there is the emotionally absent father. He is physically present in the home and may even provide financially for the family. Although physically present, he is uninvolved in the daily lives or activities of his children. He probably has his own hobbies that turn his focus elsewhere. He leaves the development of the child to the mom. He makes no attempt to show true unconditional, *hesed* love with his children. He is truly emotionally detached from the lives that are in his realm of responsibility.

The last father is the father who is abusive. His words are harsh. He is intense and his verbal tirades are a threat and fear of the entire family. Approval is hard to come by, and if it is given – it is usually conditional. This father's abuse ranges from molestation, beatings and verbal belittling, to control in any form. It is intense in nature and feared by all.

Sylvia Gunter shared with me that for many years she believed that while all three types of the fathers listed below are damaging to a person, there is one that in her opinion is by far the worst. Years before she had believed that the two most damaging father images were the absent father and abusive father but as she ministered to women she discovered that the most damaging father was the emotionally absent father. He was there but he wasn't. You see children of the other two types of father's could easily see that their fathers were bad examples of the heavenly Father. They could forgive this earthly father. Then they could receive healing from the heavenly Father and begin the journey of discovering the heart of the heavenly Father for them. They more easily accepted the fact that this heavenly Father would take care of them and provide for them and even more easily accepted the discipline of our heavenly Father – He is doing it for their best.

But the emotionally detached father left confusion for this woman because she usually had her physical needs met but she became blurred on the area of emotional stability in her relationship to her father. She, if you consider logically, was able to acknowledge her heavenly Father as a provider but not an intimate heavenly Father that really cared about how she felt and what she wanted to be or even how she needed to experience his love in the most difficult days of her life. She probably tried to receive his love in various ways growing up. She turned to performance in all different ways and usually felt she never satisfied her Father. She might even believe if she just had been prettier, thinner, better at sports, better at..... he would have loved her and shown it. Therefore, she goes on a quest looking for Daddy love.

It is important for us to know our heavenly Daddy because

in truly knowing him as this kind of Daddy we can stop looking everywhere else for the one true love of our lives.[17]

Lessons Learned About who my Daddy is

I was teaching a class on prayer. In the class there were many women in different places of their spiritual journeys and from varying religious denominations. Everything in the class went smoothly until we came to this teaching of knowing our Heavenly Father as our Daddy. There were women in the class that could not accept that we could cry out to our Heavenly Father as our Daddy. They in fact, left the class, because as one told me, "I only have one daddy and he is still alive on this earth." I am not angry. I am not hurt by those words personally. I am saddened that these women will not look at the privilege of knowing our Creator in the image and with the intimacy with which He desires for us to know Him.

I do not want to be misunderstood and "humanize" the Father to the point that we do not understand His deity. From the beginning of time, in the Garden of Eden, when God walked with Adam and Eve, and they knew nothing of their nakedness, His desire has been for deep intimacy with His highest most precious creation. He is holy. He is the judge. He is distant because of who He is yet He is also personal. He is intimately acquainted with every thought I have. He knew that there would be the fall in the garden and that He would provide a way through Jesus Christ His Son for us to once again have the intimacy that He planned from the beginning of time. Because of our adoption into the family, we have all the rights of a daughter. I can know Him as my Daddy. He will never make a mistake. He will always make the right decision for me and when He has a conversation about me with Satan it will not be for my calamity, but for my good and for His Glory!

I was speaking at a great church in Gadsden, Alabama. I had been seeking the Lord for His word for these precious women. I knew I was to teach on the Father's heart. I knew that I was to communicate the right that we have to call him our Abba, Daddy! I did a search on my computer with the Bible study software that I have and I discovered that the same language for "Abba" was used in the Greek when Jesus was found in the Garden of Gethsemane praying to His Father (Mark 14:36) as in Romans 8:15 and in Galatians 4:6 when we are told that we have been given the spirit of adoption and by it may cry out, "Abba, Father".

As I did more research it came to me that Jesus our Savior and brother, by right of adoption, used great passion in the garden when He asked the Father to let the crucifixion pass from Him. Then I discovered that the same intensity in the language is used for the Romans scripture and the Galatians scripture challenging me that you and I can cry out with passion when life is unbearable. When we can't breathe we can cry out, Abba! We can cry out when we feel as if we have been gut kicked and thrown down on the ground. We can cry out when we are about to go through something that unless our Abba goes with us we will not be able to go. Because of our adoption we have all the same rights as daughters to talk with our Daddy with passion, and feeling, and hurt, and anger, but we must realize that with the gift and privilege of this adoption comes a responsibility to respond as our Savior did "*.... yet not what I will, but what You will." (Mark 14:36)*. In order for us to move forward and fortify our lives for the trials and suffering that will come we must deal with the issues that have marked us before this time. We must look at our hearts. We must look at our families and deal with any pain that was inflicted. We must stop cutting off surface fruit and deal with the roots. If we refuse to allow our Daddy into the dark areas of our hurt and pain, then we will be struck down or destroyed. We will want to quit. We will sink deep into depression and not return. There are a multitude of possibilities. You could name them for your situation or life. The enemy will win! I do not want Satan to win. Do you? So read on. Let's deal with what we need to so that we can be all that our Daddy desires us to be.

Mark 14:36

[36] And He was saying, "Abba! Father! All things are possible for You; remove this cup from Me; yet not what I will, but what You will."

Romans 8:15

[15] For you have not received a spirit of slavery leading to fear again, but you have received a spirit of adoption as sons by which we cry out,

"Abba! Father!"

Galatians 4:6

⁶ Because you are sons, God has sent forth the Spirit of His Son
into our hearts, crying, "Abba! Father!"

Chapter 7

Deal With It or It Will Deal With You!

In a world where women come to the end of their ropes on a regular basis there is a need for them to deal with the ever rising coping mechanisms that they use to get through the next crisis. The modern woman today uses anger (rage), seclusion (she retreats), shopping (she spends more than she), seeking all of her advice from friends (she needs everyone else's approval before seeking God), activity (she stays so busy she never deals with the core issues) and finally just giving up and saying, "It's not worth it!!!!! I quit! I'm through! You can have it!"

In this chapter we begin to look at some core issues of deep woundedness that would bring us to the point of giving up. You might hesitate to examine this area of your life. I know from first hand experience and the Word of God that hidden areas of sin in your life are deadly. When not dealt with they will rise up during a crisis or trial in your life and wound you andothers again and again. With each occurrence the wound becomes more pronounced and deeper until you become suffocated by the pain. The pain is so intense that we believe we cannot hear from our Father. In the direst of trials and suffering we believe that He has left us and we doubt His love for us. Our cries of anguish are from the depths of our beings! The cries are from a woman who desperately wants to be the woman God wants her to be, but cannot reconcile the silence of heaven. This is where I believe that we find Job's wife. I believe that today there are many women like her living in this place of woundedness.

I have found that most of us when faced with trials and suffering are no different than Job's wife. We get angry. We become wounded and we have no reserves of living water let alone an overflow. Living water is how Jesus described our spiritual birth in John 3:5. First be born of water and then of the Spirit. As with the woman at the well in John 4:14 Jesus said, *"but whoever drinks of the water that I will give him shall never thirst; but the water that I will give him will become in him a well of water springing up to eternal life."* According to Proverbs four verse twenty-three, the heart is to flow over with living water. The water is the Word of God changing our hearts and our lives and over flowing to change the lives of other's whom we come into contact with. Sometimes there is a lot of other stuff in our hearts besides the wellspring of life water called the Word of God. Therefore, when trials come our way, our well is dry or it either poisoned by liquid that was never intended to be in the well. But, if we have filled our hearts with the living water, when the trials come you and I have resources to draw upon. And if the Lord calls us to wait or the trial and suffering is long, we can know the truth of *Psalm 27:13-14 (NASB95)* [13] *I would have despaired unless I had believed that I would see the goodness of the LORD In the land of the living.* [14] *Wait for the LORD; Be strong and let your heart take courage; Yes, wait for the LORD.* Or as Job declared, *"Even if you kill me, I will place my trust in you."* We must go to the hidden places of our hearts and cry out for our God to heal us and to make us whole.

If we will deal with the deep heart issues in our lives we will be able to hear the Father so much clearer and understand His heart for us. We will be able to face trials and suffering in our lives not as one to be endured but as an essential growth process of life. God will be able to have His way through our trials. We will learn that because of what we know of our Daddy and what we have discovered in unhindered worship (intimacy) with Him we are not only going to endure and survive but we can thrive in the darkest days of our lives. We get to choose. What choice will you make with your wounded heart?

The Brokenness and Darkness of Your Heart

Like Job, have you ever been broken hearted to the point – like Job – you just wanted to die? Have you ever been betrayed, abandoned, rejected, abused, slandered, ridiculed, violated, or disillusioned? In today's fatherless generation we find women like ourselves who are desperate for the things of a Daddy God, but feel inadequate to grasp the concept that a good loving God will allow our hearts to be broken as they are. Psalm 46:10 says, "Cease striving and know that I am God." The Word picture of this Psalm is for the person to let their arms hang limply down by their sides with their heads turned upward while an all out war rages around them. Women find it hard to grasp the concept of being still. We do not understand that to be still will allow the Creator of this Universe to heal our broken and wounded heart.

When we do not allow our broken heart to be healed by a loving Daddy God our broken heart stays wounded. A Wounded heart is fertile ground for more wounding. When we have a deeply wounded heart we will have explosive emotions. Anger, rage, bitterness, wrath, course talk, yelling, screaming and fit throwing are parts of a deeply wounded and darkened heart. You can name your own darkness, but the previous list will help get you started. We need to realize that our relationship with God will have difficulty maturing if we harbor these explosive, emotional sins. We can try and justify the emotions by declaring the reason for our woundedness. God knows that there is nothing good or eternal that comes from these kind of destructive emotions. He would have us bring the light of His Word to these emotions and compare our reactions to His standard and not our own.

One of the many fruits of our woundedness is bitterness. This emotion has deep roots and when the roots sprout a plant of bitterness, then fruit is produced and many are defiled. *(Hebrews 12:15)* Bitterness affects everyone you come into contact with. It causes your perspective to be skewed and narrow. You look at everything through the poisonous fruit of bitterness. It impacts your response to small criticisms. It will cause you to be over sensitive. The fruit of bitterness moves you to become suspicious of everyone. A bitter person is easily angered. It will harden your heart and cause you to become cold and unfeeling in areas where you had been soft and pliable. It destroys close relationships. The fruits of bitterness are anger, rage, unforgiveness, hatred, envy, loneliness, and on and on…. The sin of anger can stand-alone but generally if you find anger, bitterness comes with it. Anger causes us to make harsh judgments against others and ourselves. It takes many forms. We see anger expressed when we drive our cars, when we have a disappointment, when someone betrays us, or rejects us. Anger comes from abuse of any kind. We become angry when our lives don't turn out the way we thought they would. Anger comes when we wait too long for our answer to a prayer. It comes from waiting period. There is anger when we have devoted our hearts and our lives to something or someone that then fails us or leaves us disillusioned. It comes with great loss and death. Anger is manifested in our physical bodies through illness and depression. In James chapter one verse twenty we are told that, *"the anger of man does not accomplish the righteousness of God."*

You might feel that you are justified in your anger. The actions of others that have been perpetrated on you have caused you to rise and say, "Enough, I don't have to take this anymore!" You are right. You do not have to take it, but you can't hold on to anger. Anger and bitterness stifle life for us. These two emotions suffocate us, with no chance of surfacing for air. They will destroy you from the inside out.

I have just finished reading, the New York Times Best Seller, *"The Shack"*. There are many opinions and debates concerning this book in the Christian world, but there is a chapter in the book concerning Mackenzie Phillips and his anger, bitterness, and judgmental spirit that is a great word picture for dealing with these devastating emotions of unforgiveness, anger, and bitterness. In the book, Mackenzie Phillips feels that he is justified in his anger toward many who had impacted his life with much pain and suffering. His self-justified anger was most intense toward His God. His anger simmered below the surface of his emotions. He generally kept it in check and was able to judge others without having to express himself verbally. His relationship with God was strained because of His deep pain. He had little trust in people and less trust in God.

"Mack" finds himself in a place of darkness where the anger and judgmental emotions that have ruled him are put to the test.

Through a series of questions and answers "Mack" discovers that he is to pass judgment on "God and the human race."[18] He comes face to face with the reality of how he has lived a life of judging others. He does not want to be the judge. His unresolved anger is rising as he is questioned concerning the events of his life that caused him so much pain and agony. He explodes in judgment and anger as he declares the failure of God to deliver him and his loved ones from the pain and anguish of their lives.

"Mack" is then told that if he can make this judgment of failure on God then he "certainly can judge the world."[19] He is to choose two of his children to spend eternity in hell and three of his children to spend eternity in heaven. He can't believe what he is hearing. He can't make that choice. He loves them each individually. The climax of this section of the story follows:

"I can't. I can't. I won't!" He screamed, and now the words and emotions came tumbling out. Finally he looked at her, pleading with his eyes. "Could I go instead? If you need someone to torture for eternity, I'll go in their place. Would that work? Could I do that?" He fell at her feet, crying and begging now. "Please let me go for my children, please, I would be happy to...Please, I am begging you. Please...Please..."[20]

We are not unlike Mackenzie Phillips. Life hurts us. Trials and suffering comes and we store up our anger and rage toward others. We have to blame someone. We make judgments against those who have wounded and hurt us. We condemn them for what they have done to cause so much pain. Our justification is that they deserve it. We would never do what they have done to us. We become bitter in our anger and judgment. God is not doing anything so we must make it right ourselves. We feel justified in expressing our anger in any way that we want.

The sad fact is that we are being eaten alive by our own anger, bitterness and judgment. We use all of our emotional energies in our anger and self-justification. Yet when time goes by we have no real resolution. What we need is love, forgiveness, and restoration. We demand grace from others and from our God for ourselves, but not for the people who have wounded us. We want them to get what they have coming to them.

God's word to us is that He loves us individually. He paid the highest price for the judgment of our sin. He gave His only Son Jesus. He understands the broken and wounded heart perfectly. He has nothing to do with evil and His desire has always been that we would not live in darkness, brokenness or woundedness. God knows each of our hearts, and He is not deceived.

The heart of the matter

In Jeremiah chapter seventeen verse nine it says, *"the human heart is most deceitful and desperately wicked"*. It goes on to say, *"Who really knows how bad it is."* The master deceiver has lulled us into blame shifting. *"It was my childhood. It was his fault. If she had not said this about me or if he had loved me as he should. If they would have, could have, should have...."* I am not suggesting that you have not been wronged or hurt. I am stating that God requires each of us to deal with the responses of our hearts in light of our relationship with Him. His desire is for all of our emotions and responses to be surrendered to Him.

When we meet with our Daddy God, He isn't going to say, "I know that you have been acting up and being disobedient and having anger, unforgiveness, resentment, bitterness, and hatred in your heart. I know that everyone has been mean to you. That's ok; you go ahead keep feeling the way that you are. Those people have not done you right, and I know you have a right to feel the way you do. You just keep being who you are and you know what – it's going to be ok."

The God of this universe who loves us will never allow us to stay in sin. Neither will He force us to make the changes that will lead us to true freedom and a life of peace and wholeness, despite our circumstances. When we come to Him with our hurts He might say something like, "If you will get honest with Me, If you will allow me to show you where you are deceived then we can move forward into a deeper relationship. I will heal your wounded heart. I will clean up all the mess. I will fill you with my love. I will set the brokenness straight. I will protect you. I will deliver you. I will restore you. I will give you peace. I will help you. I will calm your spirit. I love you. I really love you. I can pour into your heart Living Water. I will give you my Peace. It is never ending and ever present. I will not forsake you. I will not reject you. I will never turn my back on you. I love you. I really love you. You have to get honest first. I am waiting. I have been waiting. Come to me. I know you are weary. I know your feelings better than you do. Trust me, I Love you with an everlasting, never-ending, covenant binding, unconditional love. You are my child and I am your God. Listen to me. Stop defending yourself. Stop deceiving yourself. I am here, waiting."

The Choice of the Heart

I have discovered that life as a Christian woman is about learning to die one death after another. We do not want to die to our own rights. But if we are going to complete this life, which is full of trials, sufferings, and unfairness and pain then you and I are going to have to learn to die to our own rights. This flies in the face of everything we are taught today. But it is truth. And the most important news is that when we learn to die - then we begin to really live. I am not talking about the physical life. I am speaking of the life abundant that our Savior came to give us in John 10:10. The first part of that verse tells that the "*thief comes to steal, kill and destroy...*"What is your "thief"? I am tired of being stolen from.

In Romans 12:1-2 it says, in the New Living Translation, *¹ And so, dear brothers and sisters, I plead with you to give your bodies to God. Let them be a living and holy sacrifice—the kind he will accept. When you think of what he has done for you, is this too much to ask? ² Don't copy the behavior and customs of this world, but let God transform you into a new person by changing the way you think. Then you will know what God wants you to do, and you will know how good and pleasing and perfect his will really is.* You and I have a choice to let our Abba, Daddy God transform us into women who give life to everyone we encounter. I know it has cost you much, but don't you want to know Him more? Or do you want to be the judge? Who is going to hell because of your heart today? Job and his wife had every earthly right to curse God and die. We know that Job never did.

Job didn't stop believing in the goodness of his God when He didn't understand the plan. Job's wife shrunk into the background possibly because of her pain. Job did not stop believing. He did ask a lot of hard questions. Job asked questions like why God was silent and seemed distant from him. At the end of all of the religious rhetoric from his friends and a young man named Elihu, who had probably been listening to the conversations of Job and his friends, God spoke up. I believe everyone, not just Job, was taken by surprise by the fact that they really didn't know all that they thought that they did about God.

Only God really knew Job and his wife's heart. Only God knows your true intentions and the reasons for your actions and woundedness. When God finally spoke he did not speak gently to Job but spoke out of a whirlwind. (Job 38) He spoke about all of the knowledge that had been expressed about His nature and who He was. He then instructed that Job needed to be a man and instruct God. His discourse over the next several verses asked questions like, where was Job when He laid the foundation of the earth (Job 38:4) and caused the dawn to know its place (Job 38:12). He asked the question of Job if he had entered the storehouses of the snow. (Job 38:22) God continued to speak about nature and who raised the mountains from the depths of the seas. He wanted to know if Job had put the stars in the sky, or if he had ordered the constellations. Did Job command the hawk or the eagle to fly? Job answers the Lord and said that he knew that he was insignificant and that he would be quiet. (Job 39-40:1-5) God continues to speak about His mighty power. He speaks of His powers to bring anyone who is proud to humility and to tread down the wicked where they stand and that his own right hand can and could save. (Job 40:6-14) He then speaks of the mighty animals of creation including the great sea monster in Job forty-one. God's purpose is for Job to understand and for us to understand that He has a purpose much higher than ours. He is the creator. We are not. Job got the message. In Job chapter forty-two we find Job's repentance. *"I know that You can do all things, And that no purpose of Yours can be thwarted….."* At that moment Job understood that there was a higher purpose in all that he was experiencing. He repented in "dust and ashes". At that moment God moved on behalf of Job.

The Deliverance began by God dealing with Job's friends. God specifically spoke to Eliphaz, Job's first friend and said, *"My wrath is kindled against you and against your two friends, because you have not spoken of Me what is right as My servant Job has." (Job 42:7)* God was not happy! He instructed Eliphaz and the others to take for themselves seven bulls and seven rams and take them to Job to offer up a burnt offering. He told him that Job would pray for them and that He would accept the offering from Job, but not from them. At least these men responded in wisdom. They did as they were told. Job did as he was instructed and the Lord accepted Job.

Job dealt with his own heart first and then he prayed for his friends and the Lord restored the fortunes of Job by twofold. He had twice as much when the trial was over. I believe it is because he made a choice of the heart to let God be God and to forgive those who had wronged him. I believe we see a man who says in his heart, "I am not God and I will let God be God in my life no matter what happens to me or how unfair it seems to me."

I have not understood many trials in my life. I have felt that some were unfair. But I will tell you this, I have grown through my trials and suffering. I am not the same woman anymore. Praise God I am not the same! You and I have a choice to continue to allow the God of this universe to change us through the trials and sufferings, or we can just quit.

We are not told that Job got a new or different wife. So therefore I will assume that Job's wife was restored also. They had seven sons and three daughters. The children were not merely replacements of the children that she lost, but God showing her that she was blessed as a woman. In the culture of the day, it was considered to be highly favored by God to have many children - especially if they were male children. Note the difference in Job forty-two, Job's seven sons were not named, yet we are told in verses fourteen and fifteen the names of Job's daughters. It further states that there were none fairer or nobler than his daughters in all the land and that Job gave them an inheritance among their brothers. This was not done in the day and age of Job where women were not valued as highly as men. But Job and his wife were changed people after the trial. Therefore in God's deliverance and restoration He also blessed Job's wife in her community as she had ten more children. The two of them were blessed and restored beyond what they could have imagined. God is involved in every detail of our lives as He was with Job and his wife so He is in ours.

I do not want life's trials to settle the issue of how my life will end. I want the God of this universe to use the trials and suffering of my life to make me more of what He wants and to bring glory to His name. It truly is a choice of the heart.

The Steps to Dealing with it

First, We need to repent. The word repent is a word that the Merriam-Webster's Collegiate dictionary defines as a feeling of regret or a change of mind. In the Old and New Testaments the word repent means to change one's mind or to turn back or return. We must return or as someone taught me a long time ago – make a U-turn and start a new way of thinking. It will be hard to repent if we never admit we are wrong. Part of the struggle in dealing with the woundedness of our hearts is that someone else has wounded us and we do not want to look at ourselves. We just want to focus on the other person. The truth is clear we deal with our own hearts before a Holy Daddy that is waiting for us to return and start a new way of thinking. I love the scripture in Acts chapter three verse nineteen: (*The Message*)[19] *"Now it's time to change your ways! Turn to face God so he can wipe away your sins, pour out showers of blessing to refresh you,*

The next step is to forgive. We have to forgive those who have hurt us, wounded us, or sinned against us. This is probably the hardest step in the human soul. Women have a tendency to hold on to everything that affects us emotionally. Most women can remember with clarity the events that affected their hearts from the time that they were little girls through adulthood. But if we are going to be all that God wants us to be, then we must forgive others. Beth Moore has said that unforgiveness is like dragging the weight of a dead body on your back. That dead weight will get really heavy after awhile. Unforgiveness keeps us from moving on in our walk with God and in life in general. We carry the pain and anguish of the event everywhere we go. And when we least expect it or when something else happens all of the pain and anger from the unforgiveness comes pouring out. Usually we spew it out on anyone that is around us. It might be that we are in another difficult time in our lives and we not only have the anger, bitterness, and unforgiveness of the event we are dealing with but we further complicate it by adding all of our old stuff on top of the present difficulty.

While the aforementioned is bad enough the Word of God is the final answer about unforgiveness. Have you noticed that if you have carried unforgiveness around with you for a while that you feel even more distant from God than ever before? There is a reason for this. We find it in the book of Matthew when Jesus has sat down on the mount (a small hill) and begins teaching what we call the "Sermon on the Mount". In chapter six of Matthew Jesus has just been teaching the disciples and the crowd how to pray when He interjects something that we often times look over as Christians. He tells us that we have to forgive others who have offended or sinned against us if we want His Father- our Father- to forgive us of our sins. As we read further, He instructs those listening and us as we read that if we will not forgive others then His Abba /Our Abba will not/cannot forgive us.

Fore some, I understand that this is hard to swallow and even repulsive enough to make you want to throw the book across the room. I understand that some of us have had things happen to us that we might scream, "Do you mean I have to forgive that person of doing that thing to me!" "I can't!" "I won't!" "You don't understand what happened! What he/she/they did?" As I write this I know that there are things that have happened to some of you that words cannot even describe. I am even more convinced that our Father knows well what has happened to you, and He desires to heal you. But He knows that you have to forgive this person or persons in order to move forward in a pure unhindered relationship with Him.

Forgiveness is not about validating what the other person has done to you. What is true forgiveness anyway? Forgiveness is a release of the people who have a hold on your life in regard to an action or words that have been acted upon or spoken to you. It is in my opinion, the act of releasing completely, those who have a hold of your emotions. Usually, they have no idea that there is this emotional hold on your life. They are not thinking of you but just living their own lives the best they know how. In a lot of situations, the people are completely unaware of your feelings. But we get stuck in the actions or words spoken to us and we hang onto the woundedness and we nurse the hurt in our hearts. Unforgiveness is fertile soil for bitterness, rage, and hatred to grow.

In many cases the persons do know what they have done and there is pride and anger or even denial in admitting their own wrong. They have a hold on the person's life that they have wronged and frankly they do not want to be exposed. Usually, they point the finger back at the person they have wounded by lying and manufacturing false accusations against whom they have wounded to deflect the attention from their own guilt.

Maybe you find yourself in the situation of working through forgiveness toward someone that has physically died. There is no avenue to show or offer forgiveness because the person is not physically available. Forgiveness is not about having the person physically on this planet. Someone has said that the mark of true forgiveness is that when you hear the name of the person, who has caused you such pain, your blood pressure doesn't go up. In light of what God's Word tells us, we have to forgive in order to be free to move on in our lives and in order to develop an intimate relationship with our Abba Father. Forgiveness is the key to emotional health. Forgiveness is the key to moving on in our lives with our Abba. Forgiveness is the key to allowing the Spirit to flow through us completely. Forgiveness is saying that no sinful act or sinful words will define us. Only our Abba will define who we are. This means that for some reading this book they will have to stop right here and right now and pray a prayer of release and forgiveness for someone who has wounded them deeply. God will honor this and He will help you so that you can move on in your relationship with Him.

Forgiveness is the act of releasing the offense perpetrated against you to the Father. It is releasing all of the wrong and casting it off to your Abba Daddy God. It is saying, *"By Faith, I forgive _____ for _____ ."* You fill in the blanks. God will help you walk in forgiveness for others if you ask Him to. There are some offenses and wounds that will be hard to forgive, but He will be there to help you if you cry out for Him to do so. He will not make you forgive, but He will help you forgive if you give Him permission and submit to His will for your life.

Did you notice I did not tell you that you had to go to the others to let them know that you had forgiven them? I believe you only need to do this if God moves in your heart to do so. This type of renewal and restoration has to be bathed in much prayer. When you have prayed and asked God about His timing for this to happen, He will reveal to you the perfect time. If you are unsure whether or not you are to go to the person/persons, seek out some Godly counsel about this important time of reconciliation. Forgiveness is not saying that you have to have a perfect relationship with the person. In some situations, this will be impossible this side of heaven. But when you have perfectly forgiven someone you will not mind seeing them if you meet on the street or should pass in the mall. It means that when you have perfectly forgiven them you will want God to bless them and to speak to them. You will desire for God to prosper them and if they do not know Him your ultimate desire will be that they come to know the Savior as their own.

The third step is to submit to God's plan. We must submit our entire lives to God's plan. We generally do not like the word "submit". We struggle with it because we believe that we will lose our own way when we submit to the plan of our Lord. The truth is His plans are better than ours every time. We will never see the whole picture. We must learn to trust Him through the reading of His Word and prayer time with Him as He directs our paths for our good and His glory! His Word is a lamp to guide our feet and to light our path. (Psalm 119:105) It is not a simple, mindless task to submit our will to Him and to His Word but rather a daily, conscious effort to lay down our own agendas to the Father's leading and guidance. It takes diligence. It takes will power. It will become more natural as the years go by if you stay in the Word and learn the lessons from the trials and sufferings that He allows in our lives. At the end of this chapter I have listed many scriptures to help in your journey of submission. Remember, the word *submit* has at its root the voluntary placing of your life under the authority of another.

As you submit you will and must align your priorities to the plans of your perfect Abba. Remember when Jesus was in the garden, He asked for the Father to take the things that were about to happen to Him, away but then He completed His prayer by stating that His will was not as important as the will of His Father. You and I have to lay down our agendas and trust the Father's will above our own. There will be times that it will seem ludicrous to the world and even to yourself, but your priority is to seek the will of your Father and not your own. The mind that is fixed on God will live in perfect peace no matter what storm is raging. We can only do this by being filled up with the Holy Spirit of God.

The Fourth step is to "be continually filled with the Holy Spirit. In the book of Ephesians chapter five verse eighteen we are told not to get drunk with wine for it is a waste but to be filled with the Spirit. The word filled is in the imperative in the original language. That means it is a command for you and I to be filled with the Holy Spirit. It is also in present tense. This means that we are to be "continually be being" filled with the Spirit of the Lord. God knew and knows that in the world that we live in and the trials and sufferings that we encounter we can get so focused on the events and circumstances of our lives that we are filled up with the circumstances instead of the Spirit. What He desires for us is the picture of the Holy Spirit being fused with our spirits controlling our souls and then our bodies in living in subjection to the will of the Father. The Holy Spirit living in us and through us is what empowers us to make it when the suffering of this world would overpower us and destroy us. The Spirit's empowerment is what keeps us from retaliating when our flesh cries out for vengeance. The Spirit sustains us when we would faint and give up. The Spirit living in us and shining through us is what the world sees and is why others are drawn to us. The Spirit is our power. The Spirit empowers us to keep going when the natural says that we should quit!

The next step in living a life of surrender and continually putting our flesh to death is to understand that we are in a war. It is not a seen war but nonetheless it is a war. America is one of the only countries, in the world that almost snubs her nose at the supernatural. If you talk with some of our missionaries in the third world countries and what we might think would be the less fortunate or less privileged countries they will not deny the presence of the unseen war. Why is it that we will not take seriously the war that we are in? For some it is that we are too educated to believe in this type of war. For others it is that we have been lulled into complacency about the war. Still others are fearful even to broach the subject of this type of war. The fear of what they do not know holds them in defenseless shackles.

If you ask any military expert he/she will tell you that the key to winning a battle is to know everything you can about your opponent. Next and equally as important is to understand that you have to have a plan and a strategy to win the battle that you are facing. The Word of God contains our strategy. In Second Thessalonians chapter ten verses one through five it reads, *"³For though we walk in the flesh, we do not war according to the flesh, ⁴for the weapons of our warfare are not of the flesh, but divinely powerful for the destruction of fortresses. ⁵We are destroying speculations and every lofty thing raised up against the knowledge of God, and we are taking every thought captive to the obedience of Christ.* We are walking in this human life suit and around us is raging a war. It will be at varying degrees around us but it is still a war. Sometimes this war is intense and sometimes it is just the stuff we call daily life. It is a war that we must engage in, or we will be consumed by it. This war we must fight comes to us in many different forms. We are bombarded with different tactics every day. One of the strategies of our enemy will come from what we see, what we hear, what we say, and what we think. In I Peter five verse seven through nine we are told to first … "cast our cares on Him for he cares for us". The "cares" in this verse are the "cares" of this world that are pressing hard upon our backs. They are pushing us to the ground and when we cast them off it is the picture of us heaving a huge weight off of our shoulders. Then in verses eight and nine we are commanded to be on alert. The adversary, the devil, is prowling around like a roaring lion seeking someone to devour. The word devour is a word picture of being torn to pieces limb by limb. The passage ends with encouragement to know that we are not alone in our war. Others are experiencing the same types of sufferings that we are experiencing. We are told to be firm and to resist the enemy.

When I read the verses that I have just written about I see a vivid picture of the wild of Africa. I see the mighty lion ravenous and hunting for prey. I see a herd of antelope feeding on what little grass they can find. It is hot and many of the antelope are suffering from the heat and drought conditions. I picture one of them lagging behind. This one antelope does not go unnoticed by the lion that is lying in wait for just an opportune moment. He waits. He watches. When the antelope seems the weakest and the most vulnerable, he attacks. He quickly cuts the antelope off from the rest of the herd. He knows if the antelope gets back in the herd he will lose his edge, and so he is determined to keep his prey away from safety. The antelope is frantic, fearful and weak from the heat and drought. There is impending doom. The attack is brutal. The antelope is devoured and the lion is satisfied and victorious.

All too often this is the way we suffer defeat in the spiritual war around us. We are not alert. We do not know or desire to understand the enemy's schemes. Therefore when times of great suffering come, we become vulnerable and our defenses come down. We become easy targets for the lion that is prowling around seeking someone to devour.

To survive we must get honest with some friends and let others know about our struggles. There is strength in numbers. Others have suffered through similar trials and pain. All of our trials and suffering are not exactly the same but you see the enemy loses his element of surprise when we will communicate with other believers about the things that are going on in our lives. We can then begin to take every thought captive to the truth of what God says about our situation not what we have believed or what others have said but the truth. I am not advocating that you broadcast your business to the world, but expressing your fears, pain, trials and suffering within a small group of trusted friends or one "safe person" is the first step in our warfare preparation.

Put on our spiritual armor. At the conclusion of Ephesians chapter five and in the beginning of Ephesians chapter six, Paul the writer instructs the church regarding the manner in which we are to relate to one another in regards to personal relationships. He begins with the most intimate relationship between a husband and wife and contrasts it to the relationship of Jesus and the church. He reminds the wives that we are to be subject to our husbands. He commands the husbands to love their wives as Jesus loved the church and sacrificed His own life for it. Paul, reminds the children of the first commandment with a promise. It says to obey your parents and then to honor them so that life will be good and long for them. He then addresses the father's of the children not to provoke the children to anger. This statement in scripture also applies to mothers. We are not to incite anger in our children in the tone and manner that we speak to them. As the scripture unfolds in this passage in Ephesians the issues addressed by the writer involve the most intimate of relationships of husband, wife and families. Finally, Paul addresses the masters of the slaves telling them to treat their slaves with respect that we are all the same before God. His last statement addressed to the masters is that their master and their slave's master is in heaven and that there is no partiality shown by our Daddy God in regards to His children.

Please stay with me. I know that you might be asking yourself the question, "Where is she going with this? Why do we need to rehearse family relationships before putting on the armor of God and surrendering?" Because when we are not strong in our relationships the very next thing that Paul writes is most difficult and almost impossible to do. Paul, who is closing out his letter, says for them "to be strong in the Lord and in the strength of His might." Paul, who was chained to a Roman guard while writing this letter, knew the struggle with personal relationships. Through the guidance of the Holy Spirit, his own personal experiences and observation of the people of the church, Paul knew that in order to stand strong in the strength of the Lord was to first be right in your personal relationships. Let's get honest Ladies. When we are not right in our personal relationships, we will not be effective against the onslaught of our great enemy Satan. When we are not right in these relationships we give Satan an opportunity to cause even more distractions, anger, unforgiveness, confusion, and separateness.

Paul instructed the people of Ephesus to walk in love. If you and I are going to fight the battles that come into our lives and ready ourselves for times of daily pain and conflict then we must make certain that our personal relationships are in order. Then we can get dressed in our spiritual armor.

Paul points out to the reader that our battles are not against flesh and blood. We want to make all of our battles about the people that are standing before us. I want to challenge those of you that have read this far to look beyond those people who have been involved in the trial or pain in your life. I have learned that although people may make bad decisions that affect me they are not the problem. I understand that they realistically may cause me pain or hurt, but the truth is I must look past the person or persons standing before me and realize that my battle is with the principalities, and rulers, and the authorities of the unseen world. It is vital that we realize that if our personal relationships are not right then we will have an enemy attack. I am not saying that you will not have an attack from the enemy if you are right with your personal relationships. I am saying that relationships are a major avenue for the enemy to use for an attack against us. The suffering that comes from our relationships not being in order can cause great distraction and stress in life. You might disagree, but I challenge you to take a look at the last time that you had a relationship problem. Did it escalate into something that you had not intended? How did you fair with the mind war? At best, relationships are difficult, but I believe that Paul was intentional when He wrote first this scripture concerning our relationships. He continued to write concerning our warfare and our need for being fortified against our enemy Satan. Remember you are in a war. Do what you can, when you can to make your relationships right before the throne of God. When you have done all that you can in the area of your personal relationships you will be prepared to fight the daily battle of living for your Father and letting Him live through you. The scripture is full of examples of God desiring for us to be right with one another in order that we might live strong lives for our God.

There are times that you and I have done all that we can to make a relationship right. The other person is bent on having nothing to do with us. There is no reconciliation. Scripture gives an answer for this in Romans chapter twelve verse eighteen, "If possible, as far as it depends on you, be at peace with all men." Paul continues in verses nineteen through twenty-one instructing the church in Rome that God would take care of all vengeance. Our job is to pray for our enemies and to overcome evil with good. Then we can stand with armor on and extinguish the fiery darts of our enemy.

The people of the church in Ephesus knew exactly what a Roman soldier would wear when dressed for battle. Paul used this imagery to help them and us to understand how we are to dress spiritually "to stand firm in the Lord and in the strength of his might."

First we are to put on Christ from our head to our toes. Paul emphasized this in verse eleven and then again in verse thirteen as a way for us to understand that we are to put on the new woman and thereby be able to stand against our great enemy. We can have ultimate victory over him but we will battle every day until our days on this earth are done. Some days will be more intense than others. There will be days of rest. But nonetheless, we are to stand our ground. Standing firm in knowing that we are daughters of the King, we will not be moved.

We put on the truth. This is the belt that holds everything together. The truth of knowing that Jesus said, "I am the way, the TRUTH, and the life. No man comes to the Father except by Me." Jesus is the truth and His Word is our truth. In John eight verses thirty-one and thirty-two Jesus said that we are truly his disciples if we know His Word and then we will know the truth.By knowing the truth; the truth will make us free.

Next we put on the breastplate of righteousness. A breastplate for the soldier covered all of his vital organs. We are to put on the righteousness of God to cover our heart. There is not one person reading this that doesn't understand the necessity of protecting our heart. We must put on the breastplate of righteousness as the New Living Translation states it: "...the body armor of God's righteousness." We can never work up enough right living to equal the righteousness of God.

The next part of our armor is a soldier's practical piece. Good shoes for a soldier are essential. For a Christian, the shoes of the gospel of peace are a readiness signal of being prepared to go forth in the peace of Christ. Marching forward with the Good News of knowing Jesus Christ as your Savior.

The soldier that Paul knew his readers would visualize used a shield that was usually oval in nature and looked somewhat like a door. It was four feet high and two feet wide. Paul told us to take up or hold in front of us the shield of faith in order to extinguish the fiery darts that the enemy will launch at us. It is by faith that we will live out our trials and sufferings. Job even in his darkest hours, believed his God extended loving-kindness "hesed" – covenant-binding love toward him. Hebrews chapter ten, verse twelve says that you and I will never please our God without faith, but it also reads that God is a rewarder of those who seek Him. We will never extinguish one fiery dart coming from the enemy without faith. Lift your shield high!

It is important to note that the very first part of the armor is all about covering us. To get a visual the belt, the breastplate and the shoes are our coverings. We then have our two defensive weapons of a helmet and the shield. We have discussed taking up the shield, now let's put on our helmet of salvation. This helmet is the knowledge of the hope of our salvation. The head of the soldier was among the principal parts to be defended, as on it the deadliest strokes might fall, and it is the head that commands the whole body. The head is the seat of the *mind,* which, when it has laid hold of the sure Gospel "hope" of eternal life, will not receive false doctrine, or give way to Satan's temptations to *despair.* God, by this hope, *"lifts up the head." (Ps 3:3; Lu 21:28).*[21]

Finally, no soldier would be prepared without offensive weapons. The two that we have to put on are the sword and prayer. We are to use the sword, which is the Word of God, to dispel the lies of the enemy and transform our thoughts. The Sword is empowered by the Spirit of God. Hebrews 4:12 (NASB95) says, *"[12] For the word of God is living and active and sharper than any two-edged sword, and piercing as far as the division of soul and spirit, of both joints and marrow, and able to judge the thoughts and intentions of the heart."* The word is also good for teaching, for correcting and for training the woman of God for the battle and for the life that God has called her to live.

The final weapon is offensive and in my opinion along with the sword of the Spirit it is the most important of all. It is the weapon of prayer. If we are going to be sustained against the attacks of the enemy we must pray without stopping. Our prayer lives should be one long, never ending, conversation with our God. Prayer keeps us communicating with the creator of this universe through Jesus Christ our Savior and Lord. Prayer keeps us on alert and aware of what is going on around us. Prayer is to be prayed in the Spirit. To pray in the Spirit is to join with the Spirit living within us who enables us to pray and intercedes for us when we don't know what to pray. In Romans chapter eight, Paul concludes the letter by reminding the reader that as we pray we are to intercede for other saints that are suffering in the same ways that we are. Prayer empowers us to see beyond human reality and enables us to catch a glimpse of what our God is doing. Prayer gives a peace and hope. Prayer reminds us who is in control. A praying saint causes the enemy to tremble. In all of the armor we are never given a piece to cover our backs. I believe that this is a sign for us as believing women to know that we are never to be shrinking back in defeat but we are to be advancing in the war. Never turn your back on your enemy. Look him square in the face fully covered with the armor of God knowing and believing that, "Greater is He who is in me than He that is in this World".

The final step of fortifying our lives is continually resisting the devil. In James chapter four verse seven the writer states, *"Resist the devil and he will flee."* This statement is not a simple one but a command of the highest level. We cannot resist the devil on our own authority. Through the authority of Jesus Christ living within us by the Holy Spirit, we resist him, and he must leave. There are times that we must take a very strong outward stand of resistance. The battle is so intense it requires great resistance. But then there are times that a simple spoken word in prayer will pull the reins back on this old archenemy. He tries nothing new. Everything that he does has been done before. We can be assured that if we are seeking our God daily Satan has restraints in dealing with us.

Remember as with Job – our enemy was given boundaries that he could not cross. So when life is harder than you think you can bear – know this – God is not silent concerning the parameters he has set for the enemy. The exception to all of this, ladies, is if you are living in direct rebellion to our God. If you will not deal with your sin then you move yourself out of the protective covering of our Father and into enemy territory without protection. It is not God's design for you to live in an unprotected condition. He is the perfect

Father. As the perfect Father He will allow you to continually deal with the same sin until finally, you will stop and deal with it, confess it, repent of it, and ask healing and forgiveness of it. Then the enemy will no longer have victory in your life and you can pray the armor on and you can use your offensive weapon of prayer as a mighty spear for the kingdom of God.

Lessons Learned

As I am finishing this chapter I am riding in my car with my husband driving. We are driving through torrential down pours. I am reminded that these storms are not unlike the storms of our lives. Sometimes there are periods in which the storm clouds above us fluctuate in intensity. The wind is blowing, the rain is falling and the lightening is flashing and then when we think that it can't get any worse the heavens open up and sheets of rain are falling and we cannot see the road at all in front of us. We put on the emergency flashers of our cars and maybe some of us will pull over and wait until the storm passes. Then there are those of us who will blindly drive with great force through the storm with such intensity and speed that it is unwise and dangerous. In all storms, in the physical earthly kind and in the storms of life we get to choose how we will navigate them. Today as we have continued driving through this storm I am reminded that my husband and I will choose to keep going through our trials. We have learned to look at the storm around us and if need be we take a break and pull over and take refuge and rest for a while. But we have decided a long time ago not to quit. I have wanted to. I cannot speak for my husband, but I have wanted to pull over and just disappear. But I haven't. I have wrestled and fought and struggled and sometimes unfortunately repeated some things that if I had let the Savior have His perfect way in my heart the first time – that particular storm would not have had the same impact on me when once again it visited. I am reminded that rain is cleansing and purifying and restorative to the earth. The storms of our lives can be the same. They are not the gentle rains but the storms that get us to deal with the deepest darkest places of our hearts which need to surrender and to allow healing to come from the heart of our Father who loves us deeply. When the storm is ending it usually ends by becoming the gentle rain that washes away what has been stirred up by the storm. The gentle rain cleans the air and helps us to see more clearly.

This is the same when you and I make a choice of the heart to deal with the dark places or woundedness of our hearts. The storms churn the wounded places like the bottom of a lake being pounded by rain and wind. Those wounds come to the surface of our hearts and we can ask the Father to wash them away, heal, and restore us. He gently and lovingly does and when the storm is over we will see more clearly and breathe more deeply.

The sun will be brighter and clearer than ever before and we will see things from a different perspective. Things that used to be so dear to us will suddenly no longer matter. And our "Abba" will speak and we will hear Him like we have never heard Him before. The storm is here let the rain come and cleanse your heart.[22]

Chapter 8

Fill Up the Empty Places

Let's begin to move forward in the battle of fortifying our lives against the onslaught of the enemy. He wants to bring us to our knees in defeat, anger, and disillusionment with our Creator. He hates us but he hates God more. The best way the accuser knows to discredit God and to mock Him is to destroy the Father's highest creation. You and I are that highest creation. Think about it – you were and are uniquely designed by the Father. You have your own unique imprint. You are truly not like anyone else. The pattern for your life is different. It is your journey. What will you do with it? I admit that not everything in our journey has been perfect and even that God didn't intend for every part of our journey to be on the path that it has taken, but I do know he will take the broken places of our journey and restore and rebuild every last stone on our path. We have a choice to trust Him and believe in Him or to give up and die in defeat. If we choose the latter – then we need to be aware that this will visit the next generation and the next and the next and the next and the next! Exodus chapter twenty verse five clearly states this. So, if you will not get free and pursue holiness and wholeness from the Father for yourself then let the generations that follow you be your motivation!

In this chapter we are going to look at daily practical steps of filling the empty places of our souls and broken place of our spirits.

93

Our Abba, Daddy and His Son have a powerful Word for you through your prayer time with Him! I am praying for you!

Praise Your Deliver

We moved to southern Louisiana three weeks before hurricane Katrina hit the coast of the Gulf of Mexico. Our move was from Oklahoma to the east side of New Orleans. We had never lived this far south. We had never prepared or understood the idea of preparation for hurricane season. We were just trying to make the adjustment to humidity, heat and sweating. Our entire family was adjusting to the new call that God had placed on our lives to come to Seminary and to leave what we had all known.

In the days after the move, I was not praising my Father. I was complaining loudly about the move, but most of all I was screaming about all the stuff that we had. I had a dear friend that had come to help me move and to set up my new home and a lot of the time that she was with me I was complaining about how "we had too much stuff!" "It was a sin to have this much stuff," I said. God heard my voice and He allowed Katrina to take care of the stuff! *(Lesson learned: Be careful what you complain about.)*

Saturday, before the hurricane we evacuated with three changes of clothing, a few personal items and our red daschund, Oscar Meyer the wienie dog, to Panama City Beach, Florida. It wasn't bad living on the thirteenth floor overlooking the ocean. But we knew the storm was coming and the ocean outside of our windows was angry. As the hours unfolded and the storm made land fall we knew the fate of our stuff. We had no insurance for flooding and my husband had been the last professor hired. His thoughts were that he would be the first fired. But God our deliverer had other plans. The following week we attended church at First Baptist Church of Panama City. While at this Church, we were introduced to several Godly men who served on the ministerial staff of this incredible church. There was an instant out flow of provision for our family. The Minister of Music and his family made sure that we had clothes for our two girls. This family offered friendship, kindness and unconditional love through a very difficult time in our lives. The church then purchased the very laptop that I have typed this book on. They were available and usable by our God.

In the midst of great personal loss God reminded me that I was to praise Him for everything He was doing. He was and IS my Deliverer! He will continually be with me. He will never leave me. He knows where I am at all times. During the time at the beach as we began to regroup and decide our next steps, God led me to a passage of scripture from Isaiah chapter forty-three verses one through the first half of verse three: *"¹ But now, thus says the LORD, your Creator, O Jacob, And He who formed you, O Israel, "Do not fear, for I have redeemed you; I have called you by name; you are Mine! ² "When you pass through the waters, I will be with you; And through the rivers, they will not overflow you. When you walk through the fire, you will not be scorched, Nor will the flame burn you. ³ "For I am the LORD your God, The Holy One of Israel, your Savior;"*

As we were driving to Fort Worth, Texas where we would meet with the rest of the faculty and staff we received a phone call from the President of the Seminary's wife. In that conversation I shared with her the scripture passage from Isaiah that God had given me. She then reported to me that this was the same passage that God had given her husband. A week later we returned to the beach and received a check in the mail from a close friend with a scripture card dated September 6th, with the very same passage of scripture on it. Do you think that God was trying to speak to me about His presence with me? I do. He was showing me clearly that I will go through waters, but He is right beside me. I will go through running rivers, they will not drown me. I will walk through fire and when I come out on the other side, the original language of Hebrew literally communicates that I will not even smell like smoke.

In the month after the hurricane we traveled 7,000 miles in our van with the belongings that we had evacuated with. We shopped at clothing centers. We were provided food, money and shelter by many people who loved us and by strangers who did not even know us. We finally found a home to live in. It was a wonderful parsonage that Ramah First Baptist Church, located just outside of Atlanta gave us to live in for the next 10 months. Each of my children was obviously shelled shocked. The girls could not believe that God was moving them from the place they had always known to another place to lose everything and then move them again to a place with no furniture.

What no one knew was that for over one year my oldest daughter had been asking for a white canopy bed. I had told her that we would not be able provide that for her. Her favorite color was blue. The day that we walked into the parsonage the girls went immediately to their rooms. There in my oldest daughters blue room sat a beautiful white canopy bed complete with matching comforter and dust ruffle and canopy. My other daughter's room was light pink Disney princess. No one in this church knew that both of my daughters' desires of their hearts were being met perfectly, but Our Daddy God did. He was in the midst of one of the worst times of our lives as a family. He showed my girls that day that He knew the secrets of their hearts. He knew and knows the desires of the hearts of everyone on this planet. He knew where my girls were and He wanted to take the opportunity to shower them with His presence and His love. I dropped to my knees and I began to weep and praise Him.

Why am I sharing this with you in the chapter that I told you was going to get practical? Because you and I need to have a jolt to remember that He is always working for us and we need to praise Him for whom He is. He is not a God that is not involved in our lives but He is active in the midst of some of the darkest days of our lives. He is in the daily things of our lives, in the victories, in hardest trials and sufferings of our lives.

When we praise the Lord we acknowledge who He is and we shine the truth on His character that His Word speaks about. When we praise the Lord we take our focus off of our circumstances and ourselves and we put that focus on the power of our God to take care of whatever comes our way. Praise lifts us to a higher level mentally, emotionally, and spiritually. Praise holds the enemy at bay. Praise keeps our thoughts focused on our Great God and keeps us in perfect peace.

Praise Him for who He is. Speak words of praise in prayer in the morning, every day, every night, and all the time. Praise Him for His provision. Praise Him for His love. Praise Him for His presence.

Praise Him for His healing power. Sing your Praise to Him. Praise Him for His unconditional love. Praise Him for his mercy. Praise Him for His grace. Praise Him for His answered prayer. Praise Him for protection. Praise Him for not always giving us what we think we want. Praise Him that He is your perfect Abba! This is just the beginning but it is a beginning. Start praising Him right now. He is worthy. Let everything that has breath PRAISE THE LORD!

Ready Yourself for Battle

When we fill the empty spaces with praise we are ready then to put on our armor. We have spent much time in the previous chapter explaining putting on the armor of God. As we ready ourselves for the battle that we encounter daily we will get dressed every day in our spiritual armor. Almost every school day as my girls get ready to go to school we will pray either at our home or in the car. As we are praying one of the primary aspects of our prayer is that we will put the armor of God on. We start at our head with the helmet of Salvation and we work down to our toes. The important thing to remember is to understand that you are in a spiritual battle and you need to be dressed in your spiritual armor for the battle you face on a daily basis.

When we are in a trial and suffering time in our lives it is vital to protect ourselves spiritually. Many Christian women become victims of the enemy during the darkest days of their lives because they make a critical error in getting hooked on and focusing on the negative messages that can bombard your mind during a very intense trial. We need to protect ourselves from the enemy's onslaught and be ready to stand firm by putting on the armor of God. A major victory for the enemy is in the midst of the trial to continually inflict wounding to your heart and your mind. His desire is to see you come to a place of despair and the cursing of God with your tongue. Ultimately he wants you to doubt the God of your salvation. The tactics of the enemy have not changed from the beginning of time in the Garden of Eden. The great enemy of God desires to cause you to doubt the love and promises of your Abba, Daddy God. He does this as he launches mind war attacks during the trial and even in everyday living. Get dressed daily in your spiritual armor ladies, you are in a war.

Identify the Garbage and Clean out the Garbage

We were given a lot of furniture. In fact we established a theme in our home that we were to keep our hands open on all material goods. We were not to turn down an offer of anything that someone offered us. We would explain that while we did not have a need for the item immediately we believed that God would have a place for it. It happened day after day after day. We filled the back of our "stow and go" van about seven times and delivered furniture and other things to other people just like us.

I will have to admit though that some things that others gave us were just cast offs that no one could use. I became a pro at identifying the garbage items that were not going to be useful to anyone. God began to convict me that I had moved a lot of garbage into the house we had initially moved into in New Orleans. I did not have to move all that stuff around with me. That stuff did not define who I was but it was my stuff. I had held onto things that I had not used for years. Unpacking all of that made me realize the sin of it all and it embarrassed me before God.

Should we not be embarrassed about not dealing with our sinful garbage as well? During the trial of loss and suffering from our experience with Hurricane Katrina was a climax of time in which God did a deep cleaning in my heart. I had asked Him to break me and to identify areas of my life that needed to be made right. I didn't do this out of spiritual piety or pride but from a desire to be all that He wanted me to be. There was a lot of cleaning out to do. I began by asking Him to identify the sins in my life that I had carried around with me for a long time. The same sins that I had excused and dismissed and justified as that of being just the way that I was. He answered that prayer. It wasn't fun. It was embarrassing before my God. It was hard, but it was necessary.

I began to identify it, confess it and then repent of it. To identify it is to say it plainly to our Abba Daddy God. To confess it is to say what God says about it and then to repent of it is to make a complete about face and go in a different direction. As we identify the garbage that keeps us filled up with stuff that He never intended we will sometimes be repulsed. In other words, we might get really angry with ourselves. We will also be afraid to let go of some of the garbage that we have held so dear for such a long time. For some of our garbage it will be like we are removing part of ourselves. But it will be the most incredible freeing experience when we walk out the process as described before of identifying it, confessing it, and repenting of it. God will wash over your spirit, soul and body. (I Thessalonians 5:23) It will be a deep cleansing and Acts chapter three verse nineteen states exactly what will occur when you identify and clean out the garbage. [19] "Therefore repent and return, so that your sins may be wiped away, in order that times of refreshing may come from the presence of the Lord;..." Remember, your Abba Daddy God will not condemn you because you belong to Christ and the power of His Spirit has freed you from the power of sin that leads to death.

Do the work of identifying and cleaning out the garbage on a regular basis. There is a daily work of confessing sins that needs to be done. Then there are times for all of us that we need to spend a longer time before our God and give Him permission to go deeper to the areas of garbage that we have let pile up. As I was writing this book I have had to walk out a piece of garbage that has troubled me for a while. I had known better, but I had not allowed My God to clean this piece of garbage out. I had, in fact, become blinded to this area of my life. My God was gracious with me but it was very painful, sorrowful, and hurtful. Sylvia Gunter, the author of Prayer Portions has said, "If you clean out the garbage the rats don't come back." There is wisdom in this. As women of God we should not deal with the same sin over and over and over. We should show evidence of growth and maturing into the fragrant roses He intends for us to be. We do this when we identify and clean out the garbage of sin.

Standing in the Gap

When you have praised our God and put on your armor and then cleaned out the garbage you and I need to remember the others that are fighting the good fight alongside of us. Most of us have women around us that we can relate to and pray for. We mentioned in the previous chapter that part of the armor of God is the offensive weapon of prayer. For Christians our prayer life is the connection of our spirit with the Holy Spirit living within us. Prayer along with the Word of God is our lifeline to our God. As we focus on praying for others we fill our lives with more than just ourselves. We come to understand that there are many men, women, and children that are struggling in some of the same ways that we are. We give them strength through our prayers to keep going. God delights in our intercession for others. His heartbeat is not for Himself but for us. He has commanded us to love one another and to care for one another. While I know that we can pray for the sick and this is necessary, the type of prayer that I believe we are to be practicing goes beyond the sick. It is the prayer of intercession for strength and perseverance and protection. It is a prayer of faith, belief, and hope! It is for the spiritual health and stamina of fellow saints to keep going and to not give up no matter what.

Lesson Learned
Continue the Good Fight – Decide to Never Stop!

We must keep focused on our Father during this life of trials and victories. Some of the trials will be lifelong. Some will be momentary. You and I must decide that we are never, never going to give up and quit following God! We must decide that we will not allow this world or the voice of the enemy to lie to us about the love of our God and His Son Jesus Christ. As the Psalmist declared, *"My heart is steadfast, O God, my heart is steadfast; I will sing, yes, I will sing praises!"(Psalm 57:7)* You and I must declare that our hearts are steadfast. We must fix our eyes on Jesus the author and perfector of our faith.

Job did not move because of his devotion to his God. As we have stated, he questioned God. He pled his case before God. He cried out to God in anguish and frustration, but he never sinned with his lips. Job's wife on the other hand did sin with her lips. Oh my woman friend, if we will only learn to hold our tongue. If we will only learn that in our design, God knew that we would be fragile when we experience trials like Job's wife was experiencing. Job and his wife did not have a mediator. You and I do. His name is Jesus Christ. He is seated at the right hand of the throne of God making intercession on our behalf. Therefore, we can keep seeking the things that are above when the things that are below are a mess and out of our control. We can take our trials and sufferings to the highest court in heaven and there present them to the highest judge of all. Our Savior and Lord desires for us to set our minds on the things above. When we ask Jesus to come and live in our hearts to be our Lord and Savior our lives became His. Our Father and His Son will use every bit of the journey of this life to conform us and to change us into the image of Christ. In the midst of trials and suffering we have a willful decision to make. Will you decide to go forward in this journey or will you stop and allow your story to end? (Col. 3:1-4)

I hope that you have seen a pattern of prayer developing through this chapter. I have included some resources at the end of the book to help you in this journey of learning to pray more effectively and intimately.[23] As you learn to pray with more intimacy and with more effectiveness I would like to suggest that you pray the Word of God. Over the years as I have prayed I have discovered that when I pray God's Word back to Him I will be praying His heart. I will be in line with His desires for my life instead of my own. I will be more inclined to seek His will instead of my own. Praying God's word is not a new method of praying. I pray that you will use it. It will cause you to go to the Word of God for your direction instead of relying on your emotions or feelings for the words that you speak in prayer.

I was at a time of total devastation and desperation. I was sobbing. I was embarrassed. I was ashamed. I was so sorry. I was repentant. I was angry with myself. On the other end of the phone I heard, "What have you done?" I took a deep breath and out came a torrent of words in between deep sobs of deep confession. When I had finished there was a short silence and then I had a visual of a great woman of God rolling up her sleeves and going to work. She began by gently but firmly rebuking me. Then she told me to get a piece of paper and start writing some things down. She shared her heart. She shared the truth. She didn't mince words. She was not harsh, but she was firm. At the end of the time of prayer her words were, *"Diane, God loves you and you need to "BE" in His presence and stop doing."*

I am much better at this. There is still work that needs to be done. My temperament thrives on challenges and hard work. Therefore if I am not intentional with my alone time of "Being" in the presence of my Father God then my performance takes center stage. I will become empty and my words will become hollow. They will be hollow because they are not the Words of my Abba Daddy God. Life is coming at a faster speed than ever before. It is critical that you and I learn how to "BE" intimate with our Daddy God and His Son Jesus Christ.

Chapter 9

Don't Move

Christ and Christ Alone
Is to be our
Identity!

In the last chapter we have looked at a pattern of prayer that can and will enable us to stand when we want to give up. Our prayer lives in times of great distress, trials and sufferings must be our lifeline to our Father. It is during our prayer times that we can cry out with a loud voice as Job did. Sometimes our cries will be for ourselves. Sometimes our cries will be for intercession of others. It is in the prayer time that we learn whom we are and who our mighty God is. It is in the intimacy of the prayer time when we are still and quiet that we can hear the voice of our Father whispering to us, "I know where you are my daughter and I have not forgotten you." It is in our prayer time, in the moments when heaven seems silent and He seems to not be speaking that we pour our anguish out to Him and make declarations like Job chapter thirteen verse fifteen. *"Though He slay me, I will hope in Him. Nevertheless, I will argue my ways before Him."*

It is in this prayer closet you and I have the opportunity like Job's wife to curse God or to embrace the truth of who He is and stand no matter what. When we come to the end of our rope and want to give up – we as women have a decision to make. We either decide that God is who He says He is or we just throw in the towel and check out of life and forget the God who has loved us and given His Son for us.

For some the choice will be to abandon our faith and begin a new search for enlightenment that will continually leave us unfulfilled and searching for the rest of our lives. It will be the ultimate detour. God's Word for us is to remember who we are and whose we are. In uncertain days and years we cannot allow the temptations during the sufferings and trials to send us on a detour that will us lead to depression, anger, bitterness, and hopelessness.

I have wondered over the last months, as I have researched Job, if Job's wife would have chosen differently if she had had the New Testament and the mediator Jesus that Job proclaimed that he did not have. *Job 9:33-34 (NLT) 33 If only there were a mediator who could bring us together, but there is none.34 The mediator could make God stop beating me, and I would no longer live in terror of his punishment.*I have tried to imagine what she looked like. I have visualized the look on her face the "one-day" when her world changed. I have tried to understand and really think about all of the emotions that you would have as a woman when in one day you lose all in life that has given you identity. I have seen myself in the mirror of that imagination. I can remember days in the last few years when I was disillusioned, distraught, and in utter despair. I have looked at myself and believed that I wasn't going to survive. I have lived days of walking around in crowds alone and isolated. I have shaken my fists at heaven and I have cried out to a seemingly silent God.

Job remained faithful - I believe - because he worshipped on a continual basis. He had developed an intimate relationship with his Father. As I have mentioned, in chapter seven we hear him proclaim in Job ten verse twelve, *"You have granted me life and loving-kindness; (hesed, covenant binding love) And Your care has preserved my spirit (though my physical body and my soul are in anguish).*

Of course Job struggled emotionally, intellectually, and physically. Obviously we can see his struggle with the physical. He was a very, very sick man. Sitting on the pile of broken pottery scraping his boils made him vulnerable emotionally. Intellectually, Job could not make sense of why he was suffering with such intensity. He was alone, dejected and longing for the fellowship that he had once had with his Father.

How I wish that the majority of women that long for this kind of intimacy would learn what the Father's heart is for them. He desires for us to trust Him in the midst of the harshest times. It is in the trials that we discover whom we really are and how deep our faith is or how much we desire for it to grow. It is, to quote an old idiom, "where the rubber meets the road." We are not told whether or not his wife was a continual worshipper, but we can conclude that in the darkest hour of her life she was willing to forsake God and to demand, even command, her husband to do the same.

The difference between Job's wife and New Testament women of today is that we do have Jesus as our great mediator! The greatest problem that I have encountered in my own life and in the lives of other women over the years is that we will not do the most important thing in our lives when the trials become so intense. Instead of clinging harder and more intensely to the Word of God and to Jesus our great High Priest – we usually pull back and get stuck in the "what if's", why's and "it's not fair" or the blame game. Our prayers can become soulish in nature.

Soulish prayers are the type of prayers that you and I pray when we want the God of the universe to answer in our time frame, in our box, with our plan, and for our glory. When "our" prayers go unanswered then anger comes and so does bitterness. The spiral downward continues with feelings of defeat. When defeat comes then thoughts of suicide and forms of escapism enter the picture. Escapism comes in forms of shopping, overspending, charge cards, binge eating, purging, gossiping, retreating into our homes, isolation, any form of excess, and literally running away. You can make your own list of how you escape your war with defeat. What would happen if we began to focus on fortifying our lives with the Word of God? To fortify according to the dictionary means,

To make strong: to give physical strength, courage, or endurance; to add mental or moral strength to :ENCOURAGEfortified by prayer; to add material to for strengthening or enriching[24]

I pray that you will dig deep. Look at the Word of God and discover that He is your fortress and your stronghold. We will never get through our trials and sufferings in victory without our Lord and our ABBA Father. As echoed throughout this book, trials are going to come. God does not show favorites. It rains on the righteous and the unrighteous. *Consider it all joy.... James 1:2,* even when you want to quit!

I am not advocating that you walk around with a plastic smile on your face when your world is falling apart. I am exhorting you to store up for yourself a treasure of God's Word, in your spirit. A treasure of intimate knowledge of who your Daddy is and how much He truly loves you. It is and will be an act of our will! Trials are times of great purging. He only allows them to come our way to show Satan and the rest of the world our devotion to a mighty God and His Son, Jesus Christ. Jesus is truth and the only way to salvation, hope and true freedom. *"You shall know the truth and the truth will set you free!"*[25]

Many years ago there was a forest fire. It ravaged many acres of forest and much wildlife was lost or displaced. A forest ranger was wandering through the forest checking to make certain that there were no hot spots. As he walked through the forest that day he came upon a dead bird at the base of a tree. Her wings were spread and she looked as if she had spread her wings out and sat there and let the fire consume her. The charred body made this man sad. Why had she not flown above the smoke and escaped the fire. Why had she not soared high on the winds above the smoldering trees?

But here she was dead. What a waste. He reached out with the toe of his boot and gently kicked her charred remains. As he did this, out ran three small chicks, chirping in alarm. Then it all made sense to him. She knew that her chicks could not make it and so she did the only thing her instincts told her to do. She hovered over them and protected them at the cost of her life.

Psalm 91:4
[4] He will cover you with His pinions, And under His wings you may seek refuge; His faithfulness is a shield and bulwark.

Lessons Learned about not moving

I have a new friend named Leslie. She is a wise woman of God whom He has helped journey through trials and suffering in order that she might lead others through the same journey. She has led many to the other side of the pain to experience real freedom and pleasure from her mighty Daddy God. She recently took a trip of a lifetime with a special friend. This trip was nothing like she or her friend had ever done before. They were going hiking above the tree line in the White Mountain National Forest. The White Mountains are located in New Hampshire and a small part of Maine. This particular trip was an adventure because it was going to take these two women to a height of over 5,000 feet above sea level.

This area is known for such violent storms that trees cannot survive at this elevation. On the first and second day of their adventure they hiked from the Highland Center to Mispah Spring Hut and on up to Lakes of the Clouds Hut at 5,050 feet. On the second night they stayed in what is called a hut. A hut is just what it implies. They are furnished with coed bunkrooms and no electrical outlets or showers. There are separate washrooms and toilets and the electricity is limited for preparation of food and to light a common area in the hut. They were to bring their sleeping sacks, backpacks, food, a change of clothing, rain gear and a hikers light that would fit onto their head for lighting a path should they have to travel at night.

The hikers, including Leslie and her friend totaled eleven people. It seemed to Leslie that most of her new friends were fairly experienced hikers. The resume of some of them included the Himalayas, Nepal, and well...you get the picture. On the fourth day, the hikers with two guides, one in the front and one bringing up the rear started out from Lakes of the Clouds Hut on Mount Washington to hike a twelve-mile hike to the Madison Spring Hut at 4,800 feet.

The weather report they received that morning was to be cloudy and rainy with a wind of 15-30 miles per hour. The group began the hike and two hours into the hike a fierce storm descended upon them. Suddenly, this group was experiencing firsthand the effects of being above the tree line in the elements in this mountain range.

They would later discover that the wind was estimated to be gusting 75 to 90 miles an hour. The hikers were being thrown to the ground by the wind. They were reduced to dropping to their knees and crawling on the ground. Two miles from their destination one of their guides went ahead and realized that they were not going to be able to hike out of the storm. They would have to turn back and find the escape route.

For seven hours they hiked in rain, sleet, hail and wind. The temperature was around thirty-five to forty-five degrees at 2:00 in the afternoon. Leslie had a big problem. She could not drop to her knees. It was too painful. She tried to scoot on her bottom and experienced a great amount of pain. They were on top of the mountain and the ground was nothing but exposed sharp rock. She was struggling to stay upright. Against the trail there were intermittent rock formations on one side of the path and if the hikers would get close to the rock the wind could not throw them to the ground. Leslie was in the midst of her struggle to stay upright. She could hear her friend who was ahead of her on the trail yelling through the howling of the wind, "Leslie, go to the rock! Go to rock! It will protect you from the wind. Go to the rock! It will keep you stable!" Leslie knew in her logical mind what her friend was saying, but when she heard her saying this through the wind, rain, sleet and hail a peace washed over her and a verse that God had given her in the last few days came to her mind. *"10 Though the mountains be shaken and the hills be removed, yet my unfailing love for you will not be shaken nor my covenant of peace be removed," says the LORD, who has compassion on you."*26 Leslie was in a life-threatening situation. She also knew that though the mountain was shaking that the unfailing love of her Daddy God was a solid rock that would not be shaken!

The group finally made it to the escape route. A hiker's escape route is a path that is cut through the terrain in the event of an emergency or urgent need like this one, to get a hiker down below the tree line quickly. It is not a direct route. They had already been hiking for seven and one half hours when they found the route. The name of the route was Israel's Path. Leslie knew that God was watching over her. As she and the group began to make the descent down the mountain on the Israel's Path darkness overcame them.

They had to attach the lights to their hats. The light only shone enough light for the next step. A hiker's light began to fade and Leslie would have to turn at times and shine her light behind her in order for the lady to take the next step in safety. They forged streams and thick woods but eventually after another 7 ½ hours made it back to base camp.

A seven-hour hike had turned into a 15 hour hike! They had planned for a 7-hour hike but no one ran out of food or water. Everyone had the dry clothing they needed to keep from experiencing hypothermia. God had truly been with this group. Praise God for the experienced guides that could lead this group to safety from the raging storm that began at the top of the mountain.

Do you see the parallels in this true story and in some of our trials and sufferings on this earth? Leslie was being blown down to the ground by the wind. She could not hold herself up and make any progress. She tried to do it the natural way of crawling on her knees and scooting on her bottom, but to no avail. It was only when she was able to get to rock formations that shielded her from the wind could she make some ground and continue on home.

Trials and sufferings will blow us to the ground. They will suck the life right out of us. We have tried to make it on the path without going to the Rock and we haven't gotten very far down the path. It is only when you and I will *"GO TO THE ROCK!"* that we can then make some headway down the path. He is our shield from the effects of the trials and pains. He is there with us. He will not leave us.

And when we finally turn the corner and the escape route is there before us. He will be there with us too. Remember at the beginning of this book we talked about the purpose of Job's trial. God knew Job was a righteous man and He was going to use this trial for His glory and Job's good. He is for us not against us. He will give us enough provision to make it. You can trust Him. He is there to deliver us from the darkest days of our lives. He will use His Word to be like the hiker's light. The Word of God will light our path through the escape route one step at a time. We usually want to run through the escape route and just get away from all of the pain and suffering. It is in facing the pain, the darkness, and the suffering that true healing comes. It is in acknowledging that we were and are wounded from the trial and suffering that can lead us to true freedom and wholeness in our life. So go to the Rock ladies and let Him light your path home!

There is nothing that I can add to the powerful Word of God. I challenge you to read the following verses slowly. Understand that God truly is our rock and our fortress. He will never leave us. He is powerful and holy.

2 He said, "The Lord is my rock and my fortress and my deliverer;
2 Samuel 22:2

2 The Lord is my rock and my fortress and my deliverer, My God, my rock, in whom I take refuge; My shield and the horn of my salvation, my stronghold. Psalm 18:2

3 For You are my rock and my fortress; For Your name's sake You will lead me and guide me. Psalm 31:3

3 Be to me a rock of habitation to which I may continually come; You have given commandment to save me, For You are my rock and my fortress. Psalm 71:3

2 My loving-kindness and my fortress, My stronghold and my deliverer, My shield and He in whom I take refuge, Who subdues my people under me. Psalm 144:2

2 I will say to the Lord, "My refuge and my fortress, My God, in whom I trust!" Psalm 91:2

Chapter 10

The Reminder

I hope that you have heard from our heavenly Father in these pages. But just in case you have missed the lessons of the preceding pages:

1. *Develop godly best friends. Surround yourself with a network of friends that are going to drive you to your Daddy God.*

2. *Know who your Daddy is. Get to know Him through daily reading of His Word. Pray and seek Him. You will find Him and He loves you so.*

3. *Keep being in the presence of our Father. Do not equate your performance with the intimacy that He desires for you to have with Him through being in His presence. As someone has once said to me, "be intimate with God, Diane. Don't just teach about it or talk about it. BE."*

Sounds pretty simple to type these words out, but they are the hardest, most willful acts that you will make as a woman of God. You will fortify your life in doing these three things. The chapters I have written are not new revelations, but practical and basic to our faith as women of God in a world that would tear us apart. Life is unfair and trials and suffering are going to come. But if we know the Creator of this universe through Jesus Christ our Lord and we know how He feels about us intimately, we will stand and we will make a difference. Not only in giving Him the glory but also for all of those women watching us and for those young women coming behind us.

A Final Thought and a Lesson Learned

They sat together on the front porch overlooking the celebration of their children and their families. It had been a long time since the days of suffering and the great trial. She looked over at Job and watched him as he looked on with pleasure at his daughters and their brothers. He was a different man. She was a different woman. In the years since the great trial, Job's wife had been highly favored and blessed by her God. He had once again blessed her with 3 daughters and 7 sons. And when Job had prayed for his friends, God had restored all of Job's fortunes twofold.

This day as she looked at her husband sitting next to her, she reached out and stroked his arm. The scars of the boils still reminded both of them of the mighty events that caused the two of them to completely re-evaluate how they saw their Holy God. She shuddered as she remembered Job sitting on the ash heap, and the accusations of his friends, and the silence of Heaven. She cringed when she thought about how lonely she was and how hurt her heart was at the God she had served faithfully.

No longer did either of them have a need to justify their extravagant praise to this God who had delivered them from so much. No longer did they doubt His love for them and their position with Him. No longer did any man question her husband about his hidden sin. God had restored them in His time. God had redeemed the time of the trial.

The great enemy was not victorious and as usual when he loses you don't hear from him for a while. He would return later. God had known that Job would not fail in the trial. In the midst of the trial Job's wife wasn't sure about anything. She knows now she just has to be sure of one thing. God is her deliverer.

Ladies, I wish I could tell you that you would never have to face another trial. I would like to give a 1, 2, 3 formula for walking through this life of trials and suffering, but I cannot. I have given in this book some lessons that I have learned in my own journey. I have said before there is nothing new in these lessons, "Then why did I write them?" you might ask. Because as I write them, it is like a drink offering poured out before my Lord in praise for bringing me to the other side of my own pain.

He is faithful my friend. He is trustworthy. He is unexplainable. He is my God and I will trust Him no matter what! Come with me! Join with me! As I run my hand over my heart, I know the scars that are there. But you see, I know another one with scars who paid a higher price than I could ever pay. If He were before me, I could touch the nail scars in His hands, and I would ask if I might rub my hand upon his brow where the thorns pressed into his head. I would touch his feet where the nails pierced His flesh. Then I would bow and proclaim my praise to my God for such a great sacrifice.

We cannot give up! We cannot quit! We cannot allow the world in which we live and our greatest enemy to lie to us. We must not let the father of lies (John 8:44) tell us that the things that we have counted so dear are who we are and if we lose those things then we have lost our identity. Pain and trials are a part of this life. I know less now than I ever have but one thing I know – God, His Son and the Holy Spirit are my deliverers!

John 16:33 (NLT)

³³ I have told you all this so that you may have peace in me. Here on earth you will have many trials and sorrows. But take heart, because I have overcome the world."

When we surrender we....

1. *Repent – Acts 3:19*
2. *We forgive others – Matthew 6:15*
3. *We submit to God's plan - stay in the Word and stay current with God. – Psalm 119:105*
4. *We align our priorities to His – Luke 22:42*
5. *We ask continually for a filling of His Spirit – Eph. 5:18*
6. *Put on the Armor – Eph. 6:10*
7. *Resist the devil – James 4:7*

The things that mattered before no longer matter.

Living in Balance

☒ Stay in the Word.

☒ Surround yourself with praise music.

☒ Find a close buddy (someone with skin on) that you can express yourself with and who will be honest with you.

☒ Spend much time talking with God. Stay focused on Him. Be honest with Him.

☒ When you are weary - stop and rest. De-clutter your life. Listen to your body.

☒ Make a decision that you will love God no matter what.

☒ NEVER, NEVER compare your problems or blessings with someone else.

☒ Be patient!It will end when God says so. His way of dealing with our journey is NEVER our way.

☒ Finally, remember – He loves you and that will never change.

Historical Background on the Book of Job

They were real people

Although many biblical scholars would like to think that this book is allegory, written in poetic form, he was a real man and she was a real woman. The book of Ezekiel mentions him (14:14-20) and then in the New Testament book of James (5:11), *"we give great honor to those who endure under suffering. For instance, you know about Job, a man of great endurance. You can see how the Lord was kind to him at the end, for the Lord is full of tenderness and mercy."* Why would these two books of God mention him as a real person if he weren't? So I must conclude that Job and his wife and his children and his property and his life and trials were real. They were and are as real as what you and I encounter today.

Perhaps, you are reading this book and really do not take the Bible as a real viable source of lessons or that it simply is a book full of good, moral lessons that can be used as a guide for your life. You might even agree with some of the scholars that have written about the book of Job. If this is the case, I would challenge you to then look at it as a lesson you could live your life by. Ask God to speak to you about the lessons you can learn from this mysterious woman. I find it interesting that to ponder that if this story is not an actual event in our history the author of this book had great insight to human nature for today so long ago. We can come to the conclusion that as much as we have "evolved" the nature of man has not changed in 4,000 years.

Time of Job

The book of Job is very old. The dialogue section of the book is written in the most difficult and archaic Hebrew in the Old Testament. There is not one mention of the Law, no reference to Abraham or to the covenants of God. Most scholars date the book of Job probably in the time of the patriarchs, between 2100 and 1700 B.C. or 1800 years before Christ. The theme, "there is nothing new under the sun," comes to mind. Human beings nature has not changed, Satan's schemes and plans have not changed and praise God He has not changed and never will!

The place that the story takes place is most likely somewhere near the northernmost part of Saudi Arabia. It was near Edom to be associated with it and it was also close enough for the Chaldean raiders (Job 1:17).

Some things of interest

The book of Job is the first place the devil is given his name of Satan. The word "Satan," in Hebrew, means "one who lies in wait"; and "adversary" in a court of justice. The accuser as in Revelation 12:10. Satan is before the throne accusing the brethren day and night but we have an advocate – JESUS!

The two Hebrew words translated "painful sores" were used of the plagues of "festering boils" in Egypt (Ex. 9:8-11; Deut. 28:27) and of Hezekiah's illness (2 Kings 20:7, "boil"). Some scholars say the disease may have been smallpox; others say it was elephantiasis. It was apparently some skin condition with scabs or scales. This disease, as attested by physicians today, matches the symptoms of Job's afflictions—inflamed, ulcerous sores (Job 2:7), itching, degenerative changes in facial skin, loss of appetite (3:24), depression (3:24-25), loss of strength (6:11), worms in the boils (7:5), running sores (7:5), difficulty in breathing (9:18), darkness under the eyes (16:16), foul breath (19:17), loss of weight (19:20; 33:21), continual pain (30:17), restlessness (30:27), blackened skin (30:30), peeling skin (30:30), and fever (30:30).

The word "curse" and "bless" are the same word in Hebrew in this scripture passage. Gesenius says, the original sense is to "kneel," and thus it came to mean to bend the knee in order to give either a blessing or a curse. Job's wife knew this and so did Job. So, when she said, "Curse God and die", she was being sarcastic. I have always envisioned her with her hands on her hips - with a really mean, fed-up, "I cannot believe what I am hearing or seeing face," saying, "Well (with a southern twang), AAR Yew still goin to trust God after all of this - well, BLEEESSSS God and die ! " with a very sarcastic emphasis! I know this is not what she sounded like but there is no woman in the world like a good southern woman fed up with where she is!!!!!!

CAN I GET A WITNESS OUT THERE!!!! YES!!! AMEN!!!!

Works Consulted and Sited

Alden, Robert L. New American Commentary. Volume 11, Job. Broadman Press, Nashville, Tennessee, 1993.

Barna, George. The Barna Group, Ltd. 1957 Eastman Ave. Ste B, Ventura, California, 93003 United States (805) 639-0000. Phone interview, 2001. www.barna.org.

Brestin, Dee. The Friendships of Women. NexGen, Cook

Chambers, Oswald. My Utmost for His Highest: Journal, Selections for the Year, August 4th: Oswald Chambers Publications Association, Ltd. 1963.

Cloud, Dr. Henry, & Townsend, Dr. John. Safe People. Zondervan, Grand Rapids, Michigan, 1995.

Freeman, James M. Edited by: Harold J. Chadwick. The New Manners & Customs of the Bible. Bridge-Logos Publishers, Gainesville, Florida, 1998, 2003.

Gaines, Donna. There's Gotta Be More: Enjoying the Spirit-Filled Life: B& H Publishing Group, Nashville, Tennessee, 2008.

Gunter, Sylvia. For the Family. AlphaGraphics, Hoover, Alabama, 1994.

Gunter, Sylvia. Prayer Portions; The Father Heart of God, page 45. Alpha Graphics, Hoover, Alabama 2005

Gunter, Sylvia. Prayer Portions, Alpha Graphics, Hoover, Alabama, 1991.

Gunter, Sylvia & Burk, Arthur. Blessing Your Spirit. The Father's Business. Birmingham, Alabama, 2005.

Hawkins, Suzi. Editors: Dorothy Kelley Patterson and Rhonda H. Kelley. Women's Evangelical Commentary: Old Testament: Job. Broadman and Holman Publishing Group. June, 2007.

Jamieson, Robert ; Fausset, A. R. ; Fausset, A. R. ; Brown, David ; Brown, David: *A Commentary, Critical and Explanatory, on the Old and New Testaments.* Oak Harbor, WA : Logos Research Systems, Inc., 1997, S. Eph 6:17

Jamieson, Robert, Fausset, A. R., and Brown, David.Commentary Critical and Explanatory on the Whole Bible, 1971.

Lucado, Max. God Thinks You're Wonderful! Illustrations by Chris Shea. J. Countryman, 2003.

Merriam-Webster, Inc. *Merriam-Webster's Collegiate Dictionary.* Includes index. 10th ed. Springfield, Mass., U.S.A.: Merriam-Webster, 1996, c1993.

Moore, Beth. Get Out of that Pit. Integrity Publishers, Nashville, Tennessee, 2007.

Richards, Lawrence O. The Teacher's Commentary, Victor Books, 1987.

Strong, James, Kohlenberger, John R., Swanson, James A., The Strongest Strong's Exhaustive Concordance: 21st Century. (Hardcover) Zondervan, 2001.

Walvoord, John F.; Zuck, Roy B.; Dallas Theological Seminary: *The Bible Knowledge Commentary: An Exposition of the Scriptures.* Wheaton, IL : Victor Books, 1983-c1985, S. 1:721

Wiersbe, Warren W. Wiersbe's Expository Outlines on theOld Testament. Victory Books, 1993.

Willmington, Harold L. Willmington's Bible Handbook. Tyndale House Publishers, Inc., Wheaton, Illinois 1997.

Young, William P The Shack. Windblown Media, Newbury, Park, California, 2007.

Zodhiates, Spiros. The Complete Word Study Old Testament, King James Version. Editors: Baker, Warren D.R.E. Associate Editors Rake, Tim and Kemp, David, AMB Publishers Chattanooga, TN., 1994.

Scriptures & Notes by Chapter

1 Ecclesiastes 1:9 (NLT) ⁹History merely repeats itself. It has all been done before. Nothing under the sun is truly new.
2 Job 1:3; New Living Translation
3 Job 1:8; NLT

Chapter 2
When Life Seems Unfair
4 John 8:44 (NASB95) ⁴⁴"You are of *your* father the devil, and you want to do the desires of your father. He was a murderer from the beginning, and does not stand in the truth because there is no truth in him. Whenever he speaks a lie, he speaks from his own *nature,* for he is a liar and the father of lies.

Chapter 3
With Friends Like These Who Needs Enemies
5 Job 2:11-13; Holy Bible: New Living Translation
6 Merriam-Webster, Inc. *Merriam-Webster's Collegiate Dictionary.* Includes index. 10th ed. Springfield, Mass., U.S.A.: Merriam-Webster, 1996, c1993.
7 *Romans 16:18 (NLT) Such people are not serving Christ our Lord; they are serving their own personal interests. By smooth talk and glowing words they deceive innocent people. Holy Bible: New Living Translation.* Wheaton, Ill.: Tyndale House, 1997.
8 *Proverbs 27:6 (NLT) Wounds from a friend are better than many kisses from an enemy. Holy Bible: New Living Translation.* Wheaton, Ill.: Tyndale House, 1997.
9 *Psalm 119:9-16 (NLT) ⁹How can a young person stay pure? By obeying your word and following its rules. ¹⁰I have tried my best to find you— don't let me wander from your commands. ¹¹I have hidden your word in my heart that I might not sin against you. ¹²Blessed are you, O LORD; teach me your principles. ¹³I have recited aloud all the laws you have given us. ¹⁴I have rejoiced in your decrees as much as in riches. ¹⁵I will study your commandments and reflect on your ways. ¹⁶I will delight in your principles and not forget your word. Holy Bible: New Living Translation.* Wheaton, Ill. : Tyndale House, 1997

Chapter 4
The BFF Factor
10 Proverbs 18:24
11 For more information on the "hesed" and its meanings see A.J.S. Anthony J. Saldarini, Ph.D.; Associate Professor; Department of Theology; Boston College; Chestnut Hill, Massachusetts.
12 Scriptures for thought and prayer on potential alligators.
13 Alligators and Roses adapted from Dee Brestin. *The Friendships of Women.* Colorado Springs: NexGen an imprint of Cook Communications Ministries, 1987.

Chapter 5
Who's Your Daddy

14 Psalm 139:13-16 (NASB95) [13] For You formed my inward parts; You wove me in my mother's womb. [14] I will give thanks to You, for I am fearfully and wonderfully made; Wonderful are Your works, And my soul knows it very well. [15] My frame was not hidden from You, When I was made in secret, *And* skillfully wrought in the depths of the earth; [16] Your eyes have seen my unformed substance; And in Your book were all written The days that were ordained *for me,* When as yet there was not one of them.

15 Prayer Portions; The Father Heart of God, page 45. Sylvia Gunter, Alpha Graphics, Hoover, Alabama 2005.

Chapter 6
Why Do I have to Know my Daddy?

16 The Barna Group, Ltd. 1957 Eastman Ave. Ste B Ventura, California, 93003 United States (805) 639-0000. Phone interview, 2001. www.barna.org.

17 Sylvia Gunter is the author of several Prayer books and the founder of The Father's Business.

Chapter 7
Deal With it or It will Deal with You

18 Young, William P. The Shack., page 160. Windblown Media,
        Newbury, Park, California, 2007.

19 The Shack, page 162.

20 The Shack, page 163.

21 Jamieson, Robert ; Fausset, A. R. ; Fausset, A. R. ; Brown, David ; Brown, David: *A Commentary, Critical and Explanatory, on the Old and New Testaments.* Oak Harbor, WA : Logos Research Systems, Inc., 1997, S. Eph 6:17

22 The scriptures listed below are included for you to meditate as you begin to deal with it.

Psalm 86:5-7

Psalm 63:7-8

Psalm 57:2-3

Psalm 55:22

Psalm 27:13-14

Philippians 4:6-7

Psalm 37:5-6

Psalm 36:7-10

Psalm 71:3

Jeremiah 29:11

Proverbs 16:9

Isaiah 26:3

Proverbs 16:9

Romans 5:3

Psalm 37:4

Chapter 8
Fill Up the Empty Places
23 Praying God's Word by Beth Moore
  In the School of Prayer by T.W. Hunt
  Prayer Portions by Sylvia Gunter
  The Power of Praying through the Bible by Stormie Omartian
  (Numerous other titles on Prayer by Stormie Omartian.)
  Hearing God's Voice by Henry Blackaby and Richard Blackaby
  Life Changing Power of Prayer by T.W. Hunt
  The Papa Prayer by Larry Crabb
  Prayer: Does It Make A Difference by Philip Yancey
  ACTS in Prayer by E. W. Price Jr.
  Lord, Teach Me to Pray by Kay Arthur
  What Happens When Women Pray by Evelyn Christianson

Chapter 9
Don't Move
24 Merriam-Webster, Inc. *Merriam-Webster's Collegiate Dictionary.* Includes index. 10th ed. Springfield, Mass., U.S.A.: Merriam-Webster, 1996, c1993.
25 John 8:32
26 Isaiah 54:10 (NIV)

Chapter 10
The Reminder

CPSIA information can be obtained at www.ICGtesting.com
Printed in the USA
LVOW101458051011

249244LV00005B/83/P